Transnational Identities

Transnational Identities

WOMEN, ART, AND MIGRATION IN CONTEMPORARY ISRAEL

Tal Dekel

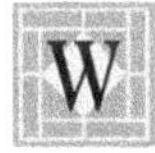

Wayne State University Press
Detroit

20 19 18 17 16 5 4 3 2 1

ISBN 978-0-8143-4250-3 (paperback); ISBN 978-0-8143-4251-0 (ebook)
Library of Congress Cataloging Number: 2016937279

♾

Published with support from the Goldman Scholarly Publication Fund.

Designed and typeset by Charles Sutherland, E.T. Lowe Publishing Company
Composed in Adobe Caslon

Wayne State University Press
Leonard N. Simons Building
4809 Woodward Avenue
Detroit, Michigan 48201-1309

Visit us online at wsupress.wayne.edu

To my parents, Eva and Ariel Oster

Contents

Art, Gender, and the Migration Experience in Israel

An Introduction

Transnational Identities: Women, Art, and Migration in Contemporary Israel is a polyphonic collection of voices of migrant women artists in Israel that reflects their individual and collective experiences of migration, in particular, the gendered aspects of this experience.[1] In this volume I deal with three groups of women artists living in Israel: immigrants from the former Soviet Union (FSU), immigrants from Ethiopia, and migrant workers from the Philippines. Although the Filipina migrant workers possess a different status from the other two groups, they have all been living in Israel since the early 1990s and share many common challenges. To lay the groundwork for an analysis of the themes that recur in their artwork, which I offer in the subsequent chapters of this book, I first briefly discuss the notions of global migration and transnationalism and then examine gender and several other identity-related categories, notably, religion, race, and class, which are important aspects of this analysis. These categories underline the complex nexus of overlapping and sometimes contradictory affiliations and identities that characterize migrating subjects in an age of globalization.

MIGRATION

The experience of moving from one country to another with the intention of building a new life in a foreign place frequently involves a sense of disconnection from familiar and accepted values and norms, resulting in a need to redefine the components of one's identity. Alongside the promise of a new and better life, migration also entails many challenges, including instability and isolation, the feeling of being an outsider, and an undermining of the migrant's familiar definitions of such basic notions as space and home, leading to complex negotiations with one's surroundings and oneself (Meskimmon and Rowe, 2013). The desire to assimilate and become part of the new society often conflicts with the need to preserve components of one's homeland culture (Ankori 1993: 97; Gitzin-Adiram and Abir, 2007: 3), and the effects of this protracted process may accompany a migrant for many years and possibly for life.

This liminal predicament, occupying a position on the threshold between a past and a present existence, evokes the notion of *hybridity*. In addition to being an intensely debated theoretical concept, particularly in the field of postcolonial studies, hybridity delineates a quotidian reality of concrete practices. It describes how individuals and communities cope with the daily conflicts engendered by life under a regulating cultural gaze that both embodies and dictates a unified and unambiguous identity. For many migrants, however, such a monolithic, rigid determination of identity is irrelevant because several identities coexist simultaneously. Hybrid existence is tentative, requiring practices of constant change and performance, each public appearance highlighting a different aspect of the migrant's identity in accordance with the expectations of a given social context. Contemporary hybridity discourse proceeds from the assumption that a stance that limits itself to binary categories reduces the full spectrum of cultural possibilities (Shmueloff et al. 2007: 6). However, hybrid subjects are often perceived by the normative hegemonic social group as posing a threat to society because their multiplicity does not fit into any one clear, fixed category. Dynamic, unstable, paradoxical, and essentially performative, the multilayered identity of the hybrid migrating subject undergoes a process of "Othering" by the veteran society. Therefore hybridity holds important political potential, for the state of hybridity opens up new possibilities for action and resistance, encouraging subversive practices and the formation of new categories of identity, especially in cases of marginalization and oppression.

Encompassing the full gamut of aspects related to migration along with the various theoretical tools used to conceptualize them is an almost impossible task. The migration experience simultaneously includes inner-subjective personal processes and political-universal facets, and the two categories are often hard to differentiate. The methodology of the present study, which integrates an analysis of artworks with a sociopolitical feminist analysis, is designed to bridge these two dimensions and demonstrate their complementary nature. Personal expressions, such as the artworks considered here, reflect and attest to the sociopolitical reality, whereas the sociopolitical reality and critical analyses of this reality deeply influence the way in which art is created. As a nonverbal tool, visual art constitutes a unique and powerful means for examining reality; it is a navigation device of sorts, possessing a sense of direction, the power of exemplification, and the ability to function as a vector that sheds light on social and cultural themes. In this sense, the artwork of migrant women artists opens up an alternative and surprising window onto their lives in general and their lives as migrants in particular.

The age bracket on which I have chosen to focus my study—the so-called 1.5 generation of immigrants in Israel—is one that captures a particularly rich swath of migration experience and its attendant challenges. In sociology and migration studies the term *1.5 generation* designates immigrants who arrived in the destination country between early childhood and late adolescence (Lev Ari, 2012: 210). In the Israeli case the immigrants from Ethiopia and the FSU, who arrived as girls or youths in the early 1990s, are now in their 30s and 40s. Like all 1.5-generation immigrants, they can be seen as a liminal group, insofar as they have neither experienced the full process of uprooting, as first-generation immigrants did, nor been born in the destination country, as second-generation immigrants were. Rather, they lie in-between the old and new worlds, their lives a distilled illustration of the formative and ongoing nature of the process of migration. This group, who experienced immigration at a stage in life when extreme transitory processes of gender identity occur (from girlhood to womanhood) and when additional aspects of identity are undertaken (such as from being Russian to being Israeli), constitutes a fascinating example of the deep and multifaceted transformations and challenges entailed by migration. Unlike the 1.5-generation immigrants from Ethiopia and the FSU, the migrant Filipina workers came to Israel as adults. Nonetheless, these women experienced a profound sense of foreignness because of their marginal place in society, in terms of class, nationality, religion, and gender, and because they are segregated also by the law in Israel, which is an ethnonational Jewish state. Therefore they too are discussed here under the logic of a marginalized, liminal group.

Although the global migration of women is a growing phenomenon that has several causes, migration takes on an added and unique dimension in Israel. The State of Israel was founded and defined as the ancestral homeland of the Jews. Jewish immigration, known as *aliyah*—the "ascension" or "going up" to Zion described in the Psalms—is a distinct migratory phenomenon. An integral part of the Zionist ethos, it is inspired by the verse "Your children shall return to their country" (Jeremiah 31:17) and by the paradigm of the ingathering of the exiles. From its inception, Israel has been an immigration state and, moreover, one marked by ethnic nationalism, insofar as citizenship is automatically granted only to members of the dominant ethnicity, that is, to Jews.

This principle, which forms a key element in Israel's Jewish identity, creates bureaucratic, theological, and political complications related to the identity definition of many of its residents. This complex circumstance is prominent in the case of FSU and Ethiopian immigrants, many of whom cannot prove their Judaism to the satisfaction of the rabbinic authorities and therefore face significant obstacles to full assimilation. Israel's status as an immigrant society of Jews alone also affects the migrant workers who come in search of a livelihood and often also support their families back home; Israel's uncompromising official policy ensures that they are denied any permanent status and can stay in the country for only a limited time.

The complexity of the phenomenon of migration in Israel is reflected in the terminology used to refer to immigrants. Jewish immigrants, whose right to citizenship is guaranteed by the Law of Return,[2] are generally known as *olim hadashim* ("new arrivals who come up to Zion"), whereas non-Jewish migrants who come seeking work are known as foreign workers. *Aliyah* carries a pejorative connotation, as noted by, among many others, Claris Harbon, a lawyer and Mizrahi social activist who argues that the terms *aliyah* and *yerida* present the link with the State of Israel as one "in which Israel is the starting point and stands at the top of the ladder, one either having to 'go up' or 'go down'" (Harbon, 2012: 72). Herein, I use the term *migrant* to describe all the artists I discuss, in accordance with the concept of global migration and transnationalism, and I use the term *aliyah* only in the context of official or public Israeli media that relate to the immigrants in the context of the state-Zionist discourse.

TRANSNATIONALISM

Western historiography tends to date the emergence of the age of transnationalism to the late 1980s and early 1990s; its key symbol is the collapse of the Berlin Wall. The age of transnationalism is characterized by fundamental changes in the nature of nation-states brought on by massive waves of migration. Because many actual borders have changed or disappeared since the 1990s, migration laws have also been altered, so that the movement from one county to another is now considered easier than ever before, although voluntary and forced migrants are facing new challenges and obstructions on their path. Immigration has become an important item on the public and political agenda of most Western states, gaining high visibility. The phenomenon has been stimulated by lower-cost and more easily accessible forms of transport, by the growing economic gap between the developed and developing nations, and by violent regional and local conflicts that have left countless numbers of people homeless and stateless. Immigrants leave their native countries for numerous reasons, among them political circumstances, economic circumstances, and the general desire for a better life elsewhere.

The discourse of transnationalism addresses the meeting points between personal migration experiences and the broader worldwide migratory movement. Anthropologists Sarah Mahler and Patricia Pessar (2001) describe transnationalism as a phenomenon that differs from globalism: Global processes occur across the world independently of specific or local events that take place in the territorial space of a particular nation-state, whereas transnational processes take place in several places at once across the globe and relate to the practices of people who are linked, physically or virtually, by family connections, economics, and nationality to more than one geonational space. Rather than purely economic and political patterns on a global scale, transnational phenomena involve individual people and nation-states. Although immigrants are obviously affected by global processes, they give them meaning through their personal acts of migration and also influence these processes in turn, leaving a mark on both their country of origin and their destination country. Unlike the discourse of globalization and pan-world processes, which focuses on a one-directional influence—typically that of the capitalist West over the rest of the world—and which tends to overlook differences between particular national contexts, in the transnational discourse nation-states and national borders remain significant elements, enriching and concretizing the particular individual and narratives of migrants (Mahler and Pessar, 2001: 443–44).

In trying to merge gendered perspectives and especially feminist criticism with transnationalism, Caren Kaplan and Inderpal Grewal proposed the term *transnational feminism* as an appropriate replacement for the contentious, totalizing, and homogenizing concepts of global or international feminism, explaining that *transnational* as a term is useful only when it signals attention to uneven and dissimilar circuits of culture and capital, revealing the links among patriarchies, colonialism, and racism (Kaplan and Grewal, 1999). Esther Fuchs (2014b) explains this stance further: "The concept of transnational feminism marks critical practices that bring the economic and governmental into cultural criticism" (4).

The events marking the emergence of the transnational age have directly and personally affected the women migrant artists at the center of this study. The FSU, Ethiopian, and Filipina women artists who came to Israel have all been affected by geopolitical changes that enabled—or impelled—population transfers. The collapse of the Soviet Union opened the gates for Jewish emigration (Galili and Bronfman, 2013). The change of regime in Ethiopia in May 1991, which was influenced by global events, including the collapse of communism in the FSU, was perceived as posing a threat to the country's Jewish community and accelerated the execution of Operation Solomon (1991), which brought the Ethiopian Jewish community to Israel (Turel, 2013). The official policy of encouraging migrant workers to come to Israel, first articulated in the Israeli parliament in 1988, was a direct consequence of the geopolitical, political, and economic changes that occurred during this period, both in the local Israeli context (related primarily to developments in the Israeli-Palestinian conflict and specifically the outburst of the First Intifada, which stopped the employment of Palestinian workers for security reasons) and on a global scale of the neoliberal globalization economy, which gave rise to massive work migration around the world (Kemp and Raijman, 2008). Thus, despite significant differences between these three groups of women artists, the logic of transnationalism and the uniformity of the historical period create a framework in which they can be discussed jointly.

RACE, CLASS, AND GENDER

One of the prominent features of women's migration to Israel is the great diversity in their origins and their migratory circumstances (Morag Talmon and Atzmon, 2013).[3] Contemporary Israel is a rich, concentrated laboratory of different types of migration—Jewish immigrants, migrant workers, political refugees—from many parts of the world. In discussing this complex reality, I use what is an essentially interdisciplinary tool: a triangular analysis that relates to three main categories of identity: race, class, and gender. This triangle reflects the standard system of analysis used by numerous academic disciplines and constitutes an important element of critical thought in the transnational age (Alcoff and Mendieta, 2007; Dill, 1983).

Race and class are intersecting categories of identity whose embedded power structures are of particular relevance to immigrants. The social field that immigrants enter in the destination country contains numerous players, predominantly the veteran hegemonic group, which strives to preserve its status by using the means of power at its disposal. The power held by the hegemony sometimes serves to integrate and advance the position of newcomers and at other times takes the form of violence and suppression. Frequently, these circumstances lead to manifestations of sexism, racism, and class discrimination toward immigrants—whether one-off or systematic—in diverse areas of life. The triangular analysis across the interrelated categories of race, class, and gender seeks to understand the social structures that promote the various expressions of power relations, both exclusionary and inclusionary.[4]

This integrative discussion rests on the theoretical and practical perspective known as *intersectionality*, which designates an approach that studies the intersections between multiple systems of oppression or discrimination directed at nonhegemonic groups and individuals. However, as I argue later, it is a discourse that not only explains exclusion and oppression but also stands to offer new insights into the positive and enabling aspects of migration, in particular the aspects of women's agency.

The term *race* captures the idea that race has real effects and implications in reality despite being a sociocultural construct rather than a biological reality. As the French feminist sociologist Colette Guillaumin wrote, "Race does not exist. But it does kill people" (2003: 107). Reifications of race can reside in unexpected places. Thus, for example, the liberal discourse against racism in effect ratifies its existence, because its diverse initiatives for combating racism (such as the prohibition against discrimination on the basis of race or the promotion of educational programs encouraging "interracial understanding" and of policies of affirmative action) all implicitly assume that race exists. Whether or not it is a "natural" category, race is deeply rooted in language and in cultural, political, and legal practice, and to this extent it is necessarily embroiled in racist social practice (Shenhav and Yonah, 2008).

Israeli society's racist manifestations and expressions conceal and legitimize themselves in sophisticated ways. This discourse mediates the complex relationship between racism and race by means of a mechanism of cultural and political constructs that has been described as "racification" (Shenhav and Yonah, 2008: 8). This mechanism takes various forms and applies to three types of racism: biological racism, institutional racism, and "racism without race" (Balibar, 1988). Biological racism assumes a link between physical, biological features, such as skin color or bone structure, and mental attributes, such as intellect or moral strength. Institutional racism is defined by its outcome; in other words, the perception of unequal treatment of a particular social group by an institution suffices to establish the presence of institutional racial discrimination (Shenhav and Yonah, 2008: 29–37). As for the modality of racism described by Étienne Balibar as "racism without race," which emerged in Europe in the wake of World War II, its manifestations are based on the assumption of "the insurmountability of cultural differences" and in this respect involve culture functioning "as a nature." This racism "at first sight, does not postulate the superiority of certain groups or peoples in relation to others but 'only' the harmfulness of abolishing frontiers, the incompatibility of lifestyles and traditions" (Balibar, 1988: 21).

In the following discussion, I give examples of all three types of racism as applied to Jewish migrant women from the FSU and Ethiopia living in Israel. Women migrant workers residing in Israel, because they are not Jewish, suffer even more extreme discrimination, particularly with regard to matters of personal status, such as restrictions on the right to give birth. In the context of migration, it is also interesting to note that race is not only an identity category but also a structure of oppression that moves and varies across different countries and spaces (Bonacich et al., 2008).

The term *class* refers to one's socioeconomic status and accessibility to resources, either direct funds or other resources that can help individuals obtain educational opportunities, health, nutrition, and so on. Class issues constitute one of the primary causes of migration and the principal cause of the phenomenon of migrant workers. Migration prompted by economic circumstances is intended to improve the migrant's economic agency, but this objective is not always achieved. Indeed, often migrants, in particular migrant women, join the ranks of a class in the destination country lower than the one to which they belonged in their country of origin. Thus, for example, a migrant whose family has assets or symbolic wealth back home might discover that she has no access or ability to enjoy such resources in her new country of residence, and she quickly becomes aware of the deep chasm between her professional skills and the possibility of finding a well-paying job. She may lose her assets and drop into the well of poverty from which it is virtually impossible to escape.

The term *gender* is based on the idea that the alleged differences between the sexes are in fact cultural constructs designed to organize human behavior and modes of thought. The notion of gender denotes not a fixed set of characteristics or roles but a protracted and mutable process experienced within an extensive range of social phenomena, from the family to the state, from our self-perception to our relationships with others. The conceptualization of gender as an ongoing and fluid process rather than as a natural steady state led to the understanding that identity definitions, relationships, and even ideologies are similarly fluctuating and constantly evolving constructs rather than fixed entities with clearly defined boundaries (Butler, 1990). Any reading of the lives of migrants will show that all genders are exposed to hardships and discrimination as part of the experience of migration. But women encounter the further prejudice that derives from the patriarchal nature of society, exposing them to additional forms of oppression, including employment discrimination, sexual harassment and the disciplining of the body in public spaces, and various forms of discrimination related to conception, fertility, and child-rearing, as will be demonstrated in detail in the following chapters.

In the study of world migratory movements, the intersection of migration with gender issues is both clear and prominent. In recent decades the focus in particular on female migration has generated a plethora of empirical findings and theoretical studies on gender aspects of cross-border movements. These studies began to appear in the 1980s and gained force after the turn of the millennium. This intense scholarship on transnationalism has unequivocally established that gender plays a decisive role in understanding the motives and outcomes of world migration and that it is relevant to most, if not all, of the facets of migration (Donato et al., 2006; Mahler and Pessar, 2001).

In the chapters of this book I show the ways in which policy changes affect women immigrants' lives in Israel. Government policies frequently influence migrant men and women differently. They lead to the articulation of various migration models and prompt migration laws that exhibit gender aspects and sometimes even impose explicit limitations on women. They also generate decisions that directly affect the degree to which migrants are integrated into the target society and affect their basic rights, their ability to sustain themselves, maintain their health, and obtain a reasonable standard of living. As a direct consequence, the ways in which migrant women take an active part in the migration process are also intimately linked to gender dimensions, including social norms and expectations, and agency opportunities (Piper, 2008: 1). The discussion of migrant women examines not only traditional gender roles, such as women's place in the family, but also the degree to which women actively participate in sociocommunal activities in the host society or make effective attempts to participate in its national discourse.

The categories of gender, class, and race are closely interrelated. The relations between them create a complex map on which the migrant women's stratification point encounters a dynamic of exclusion and inclusion and social power relations that operate on all the subjects existing in the field. Reciprocal relations exist between different structures of oppression, both in the subjective way the migrant women experience them and within the contexts of the wide social structures (Choo and Ferree, 2010). Nonetheless, in this volume I take gender as the central axis of the experience of migration, with issues of race and class resonating within the gender dimension and enhancing it: Migrant women of all class levels are subject to the patriarchal oppression of the gendered work market, and women of diverse ethnic backgrounds are exposed in the host country to sexism and sexual violence because of their gender. Some women, as we will see in the Israeli case, are exposed to overt and covert forms of gender-related oppression because their religious identity clashes with the dominant religious identity as defined by the state. Personal status (whether a woman is single, partnered, married, divorced, a mother, etc.) also intersects with and affects class variables, for example, through laws that allocate (or withhold) state funding based on personal status. Physical ability and sexual orientation are further variables that affect the migrant's relationship with other migrants and with the veteran society as a whole. These positions are held simultaneously, so that migrant women are capable of being both excluded and privileged, weak and powerful, all at the same time.

POWER KNOWLEDGE

Migration in a transnational world creates tension and conflict between power groups capable of excluding or including others—whites versus blacks, the economically established versus the impoverished, and numerous other groups linked and defined in terms of majority-minority relations. The particular types of power at play in the present discussion and their relation to the mechanisms of exclusion and inclusion are elucidated in what follows.

Any given piece of knowledge, including the formulation of texts and publication of books such as the present volume, is bound up with power relations, or in Foucauldian terms, "It is not possible for power to be exercised without knowledge, it is impossible for knowledge not to engender power" (Foucault, 1980: 52). In this study I draw on diverse sources of knowledge—not only academic texts but also personal interviews, newspaper articles and other media, and of course, artwork. This choice expresses my desire to decentralize hegemonic power and promote the public and cultural visibility of marginalized voices, but it also reflects a practical reality, namely, that there are few publications (academic or otherwise) from which knowledge can be drawn about the gender aspects of migrant women artists in Israel.

Israeli scholarship has produced many studies about immigrants (both male and female) in a number of disciplines, including sociology, psychology, social work, anthropology, economics, medicine, and law.[5] With *Transnational Identities* I seek to contribute to this significant body of research by focusing particularly on gender issues, as reflected in the field of artistic creation by migrant women. I give center place to the voices of the women artists themselves, who were invited to select the works they view as most significant and to comment on them. Between 2008 and 2013 I conducted in-depth, open interviews with the artists whose work is featured here; these interviews were typically followed up by correspondence.[6] The methodology I followed is based on a qualitative feminist research method commonly used in the social sciences; it allows for the integration of different types of knowledge in a single composition using reflexive examination. In the field of qualitative research, art analysis grounded in interviews with the artists is a growing area of interest; it is founded on "the view that a creator's explanation comprises the primary tool for understanding the work" (Huss, 2010: 318). According to this approach, an artwork is assessed not only on the basis of the aesthetic criteria of art criticism or on diagnostic criteria that analyze the artist's biography or personality but also "as the creator's way of presenting, elucidating, and elaborating meanings and content" (318).

This research is also informed by scholarship on art and gender in Israel and on feminist writings about women's art in Israel, which saw their significant impact on Israeli art history begin in the 1990s (Dekel, 2011, 2013; Guilat, 2006; Markus, 2008). There are several reasons for the lack of a committed and systematic discourse on gendered aspects of women's art in Israel before the 1990s and the conditions and features of its arrival in the country (Dekel, 2011: 150–52), but new rereadings of early Israeli women artists such as Sionah Tagger, Claire Yaniv, Hagit Lalo, Ruth Schloss, and Bianka Eshel-Gershuni, show that gendered aspects were indeed incorporated into their work. The 1970s was a turning point in taking up a gendered perspective on women's art, and feminist ideology was also gradually introduced as a legitimate perspective from which women create art (Dekel, 2012); in addition, an open feminist agenda became a well-established preoccupation in several works of Israeli women artists beginning in the 1990s (Dekel, 2011: 158–74; Katz-Freiman, 1994).

But we must remember that women's art and feminist perspectives in art are always part of a wider, more general art field, because art is, and always was, a powerful means to understand people's lives and experiences. Artworks provide us with alternative types of knowledge and perspectives that also stand to deepen and expand our understanding of the experiences of migrant women. Their visual texts are narratives that reveal their personal stories, which bear the distinctive stamp of their individual creators while also capturing many commonalities among the experiences of different migrant women (and different groups thereof). As anthropologist Tamar El Or notes, "The personal story of a particular person carries double value: it portrays a unique life, but can also, when considered alongside other stories, be placed within its public, social, and historical context. This enhances the importance of the private biography as a source of social insight and at the same time unravels social insights into a myriad of individual stories" (El Or, 2006: 138).

Bridging the private and collective stories is the feminist argument that the personal is political. This principle, the implications of which for women in particular have received more nuanced and complex interpretations over the decades (H. Herzog, 2009: 160–61), guides my analysis in the following chapters and underlies its dialectical movement between the micro and the macro level.

Indeed, my motivation for this study also has fundamentally personal roots. I was born in the United States and moved to Israel with my nuclear family as a child; thus I myself am a 1.5-generation immigrant. The themes of migration and femininity have been part of my family narrative for the past five generations. I grew up with and still return to the stories of the women in my mother's family—my great grandmother, her mother, my grandmother, and my mother—all of whom left the land where they were born and began a new life in a different country. My great-great grandmother, Alexandra Gjestvang, was born in Norway and moved in her early youth to Sweden to join her husband. My great grandmother, Linda Sundstrum, was born and raised in Finland and moved with her Finnish husband to the United States soon after their marriage. My grandmother, Irma Lindh, was born and grew up in the United States, went to Sweden to study, and, having met her husband there, stayed on to raise a family. When they divorced, she returned alone to the United States, leaving her three daughters behind in Europe. One of these daughters—my mother, Eva Lindh (now Oster)—was sent from Sweden, as a young adult, to study in the United States. There, she met my Israeli father, Ariel, and converted to Judaism so that she could marry him. After the birth of their two daughters (my older sister, Orly, and me), she followed my father back to his homeland, leaving behind an American way of life she had worked hard to achieve.

My mother's migration to Israel was a deep uprooting, and the course of her life has been a formative narrative in my own. The foreignness that was her lot during her first years in Israel—difficulties with the language, the lifestyle and customs, the indigestible food, the lack of close family and old friends, and the unfamiliar culture—made it hard for her to assimilate, and traces of these hardships lingered for many years after the move. To this day, even after her Israeliness has become an integral part of her identity, she is amicably known among Israeli family members and friends as "our Swedish lady."

My mother's legacy of foreignness has influenced me deeply. Her blood, which seemed always to carry a "virus of foreignness," flows in my veins, so that I, too, am infected with it. My hybrid identity is informed by an ambivalent attitude toward the Israeli society in which I live, and the themes of uprooting and foreignness that have been with my family for more than 150 years constitute a recurrent and central motif in my academic work and political activities and in my personal life.

This volume embodies one of many possible approaches to the study of migrant women in Israel. The concept of "difference" among women—be they differences of culture, ethnicity, class, religion, or something else—is acknowledged in this project and is marked as a positive factor.[7] This stance has challenged me to think critically about the way I present and lay out the discussion. In terms of the structure of the book, I first set out to disrupt essentialist tendencies of discussing emigrants from Ethiopia, the FSU, and the Philippines in separate chapters; I wanted to undermine dichotomist ways of understanding each group and instead chose to promote a more nuanced, complex understanding of diversity among women and to consider their "common differences." In so doing, I was hoping to present chapters such as "motherhood," "occupation," and "religion" with regard to women from all three social groups together, in an integrated fashion and in a way that would disrupt the cultural urge of an easy, essentialist categorizing system. However, because of the special complexity of the Israeli ethnonational case and the fact that this project is a first of its kind, after many revisions I have chosen to structure this volume by the countries of origin of each group of women discussed. This discussion, I hope, will facilitate in laying the groundwork for further projects that will offer different perspectives and means of analysis.

Moreover, I do not propose sweeping conclusions or presume to speak for the women whose lives and art I explore. Rather, I sketch the outlines of their lives and their mechanisms of coping with the experience of migration on the basis of the knowledge that the women artists shared with me and on my own observation and analysis of their artwork. Within the delicate dialectic between the personal and the political, I hope to make their voices heard and give concrete form to their stories of migration in a steadily expanding transnational reality. In this sense, the words of Esther Fuchs, a scholar of Israel and Jewish studies, would be accurate for this current volume: "My interest in the potential of Israeli feminist scholarship as the location of intersecting theories for activist practice rests on my interpretation of feminist knowledge as the site of social and cultural critique in its profoundest sense" (Fuchs, 2014a: 28).

The research and writing of this book has been a long, winding journey, which has taught me, inter alia, the extent to which my writing about the subject of women and migration is bound up with ethical dilemmas. As a feminist, I am aware that my own writing on these issues embodies and concretizes a complex set of power relations. These were present when I interacted with the interviewees—the women artists who generously shared parts of their personal and artistic worlds with me—and they were present when I later analyzed, condensed, and edited what they shared with me to form a book, for which I received academic credit and other real and symbolic returns.

The power gaps embedded in the divergent positions they and I hold are frequently deep and sometimes unbridgeable, but they are also fluid and often difficult to pinpoint. In some contexts the balance of power is tipped in my favor because I am a veteran Israeli citizen who lives in a major urban center, belongs to the middle class, and works in academia. In other contexts the greater power rests with my interviewees, because their knowledge of the processes of artistic production and of some aspects of the social and artistic fields that preoccupy me in this study exceeds my own, or in cases in which one of them is of a higher socioeconomic class then me, and so on. Our positions, then, are relative and flexible, with each side alternately and sometimes simultaneously privileged and disadvantaged.

More than once during the writing of this book I found myself pondering the problem, addressed by many feminist scholars, of speaking in someone else's name. Israeli feminist activist Dorit Abramovitch posted a comment on her Facebook page that aptly describes the experience of being "spoken for": "I am marking what should have been marked long ago: You may feel my pain, experience my sorrow, rejoice in my joy, smile with my pleasure—but do not feel instead of me and do not translate yourselves through me, because then you've taken myself from me" (August 20, 2012). With this bidding in mind, the most important task I set for myself during this study has been the commitment to a reflexive stance: observing the processes involved in the research, recognizing my responsibility for the way it would be shaped, and sustaining a self-critical position. For this reason, I have chosen a field-based methodology, grounded firmly in the collection of the firsthand accounts of the women artists featured in this volume. These accounts, the themes of which were largely dictated by the women themselves, form a central source of the knowledge contained within the pages of this volume.

1

Israeli Women Artists

Migrants from the Former Soviet Union

Artists from the 1.5 generation who migrated to Israel from the former Soviet Union (FSU) frequently create works that express their unique experience of being between "here" and "there." The transnational practices in which they engage include preserving links with family members in the FSU, visiting their homeland, keeping abreast of the homeland's political and cultural developments, and initiating various economic relations with it, such as import-export commerce. These practices reflect the immigrants' ongoing state of hybridity. Even two decades after their arrival in Israel, these young women are still actively engaged in the process of formulating their migration experiences, looking back on formative events in their past from a contemporary viewpoint. Many of these artists relate to the difficulties they encounter as migrant women in Israel. Others describe migration as the launching pad for a new future, stressing the positive aspects of the migration experience. Both those who formulate the process in terms of a struggle or difficulty and those who do not reflect on their position as women in general and as Russian-speaking women in Israeli society in particular. Their artworks express and help to establish their diverse views.

Although several exhibitions have been devoted to the works of FSU artists living in Israel, no exhibition to date has focused exclusively on Russian-speaking women as a way of highlighting the gender aspects of their work and lives. Numerous themed exhibitions of ex-Soviet artists have been held in Israel in recent years, including "Cargo Cult" (2012), "3 for 10" (2011), "Safe Haven" (2011), "Split Identity" (2011), "Homeland/ Rodina" (2011), "Grobman Project" (2010), "You" (2010), "Dva Parallel Lines Nikagda Will Meet" (2010), "The Strange Museum" (2006), and "Cosmo-Refugee" (2004). Several other exhibitions addressed the topic of migration in a general fashion, including "Changing Places" (2008) and "Gentiles" (2008), both of which featured immigrant artists from various parts of the world. Several solo exhibitions have addressed the subject of FSU migration, for example, Sasha Serber's 2011 exhibit at the Minshar Gallery in Tel Aviv. Yet the subject of the gendered aspects of migrant art in general and ex-Soviet art in particular has been largely ignored in the Israeli art world and in academic scholarship.

MIGRATION FROM THE FSU

The fall of the iron curtain in the 1980s led to massive waves of migration, and a large portion of the Jewish community (among other groups) left the FSU for various Western countries, including Israel. Despite Israel's Law of Return, which guarantees automatic citizenship to Jews, many FSU residents chose to move to the United States. After 1988, however, the United States significantly reduced the number of visas issued to Jews seeking to immigrate, compelling many to move to Israel. This change in policy was partly a response to pressure exerted by the State of Israel, which sought to increase Jewish immigration to Israel (Galili and Bronfman, 2013: 43–48).

The influx of 1 million FSU migrants into Israel between 1990 and 2010 substantially altered the nature of the local populace, which totaled some 7.5 million before their arrival. This wave of migration joined an earlier one, from the 1970s, composed of 150,000 Soviet Jews (Galili and Bronfman, 2013). In Israel the two groups are perceived as different in nature. The 1970s aliyah is regarded as primarily ideologically motivated; it included refuseniks (individuals denied Soviet permission to emigrate) and Prisoners of Zion, who engaged in a bitter struggle to leave the Soviet Union in order to come to Israel. The later wave is commonly regarded as motivated primarily by socioeconomic considerations.

Like all migrants, the FSU migrants who have come to Israel since the 1990s experienced many life changes, some positive and joyful, others painful and negative. Uprooting oneself from a familiar place, even a hostile or difficult one, and moving to a foreign country might be shocking. Mastering a new language, facing housing and employment challenges, possibly losing one's status, and being faced with prejudiced attitudes of the veteran society—all these place a heavy weight on the process of adjustment, identity consolidation, and establishment of an immigrant's position.

The gender aspect summons further challenges that are unique to women immigrants. Because the ratio of women to men was greater in the Soviet immigration wave than in Israeli society, the total percentage of women in the Israeli population rose (Horowitz, 1998: 368). In addition, the large number of divorced women among the immigrants was the main contributing factor to an 80% increase in the number of divorced women in Israel between 1989 and 1994 (Almog and Evdosin, 2013).

Despite the massive demographic effect of the FSU migration, and perhaps partly because of it, FSU migrants, particularly the women among them, are subject to a wide array of negative stereotypes. This makes it particularly important to give voice to the women artists themselves, allowing them to paint the reality of their lives in their own colors. The present chapter is based on knowledge gathered largely from the artists themselves and presents their perspective on their lives in Israel. Their works revolve around themes that depict the experiences of women migrant artists, including sexist stereotyping, sex trafficking, difficulties in sustaining themselves financially, their Jewish identity, and their hybrid cultural position.

THE GAZE DIRECTED ON THE FEMALE MIGRANT'S BODY

In 2006 artist Tamara Brodinsky (b. 1981) created an artist's book titled *How a Russian Woman Does It*, consisting of digitally manipulated images and various texts. In a photograph bearing the title of the series as a whole, the artist stands clothed in her underwear in an undefined space (Figure 1). She gazes directly at the camera. Lines point at various parts of her body, and their labels counter common stereotypes that Brodinsky encountered during her life as a female FSU migrant in Israel: "Doesn't drink vodka" reads the caption that points to her mouth; "Is not Christian," pointing to her chest (where a cross on a necklace might be); "Does not curse," pointing to her throat; "Is not a prostitute/slut," pointing to her genitalia; "No abusive father/husband," pointing to her unbruised

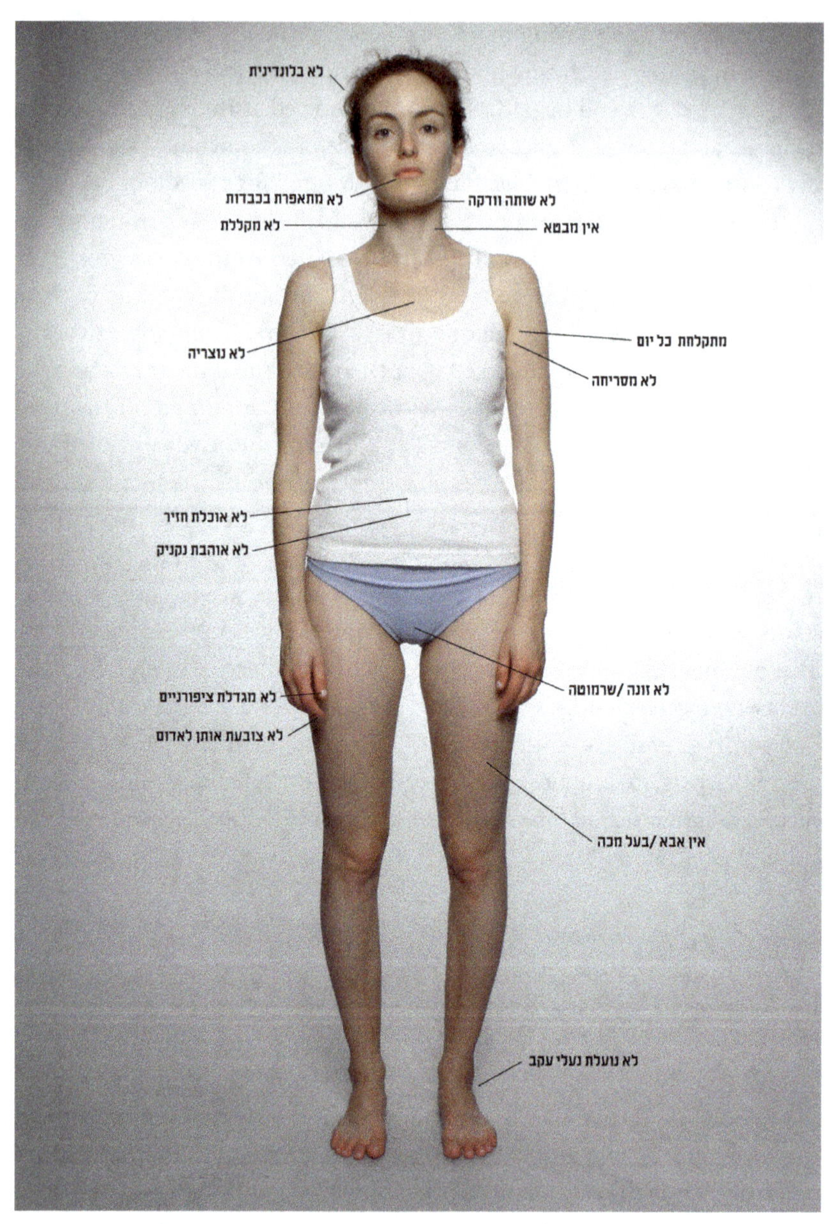

FIGURE 1. Tamara Brodinsky, *How a Russian Woman Does It* (detail from an artist's book), 2006. Digitally manipulated color photograph.

thigh. This reworked photo—and the forty other photographs in the series—reflects the views of the average Israeli regarding FSU migrant women. The multitude of stigmas concerning this wave of immigration led Brodinsky to use her own body to reflect her feelings and criticism. In effect, she demonstrates how she perceives Israelis when they look at women they call "Russians."

In my interview with Brodinsky in 2012, she related that she frequently hears the phrase "But you don't *look* Russian" from veteran Israelis. Taking it as a compliment would imply her identification with the notion that she is somehow fortunate to have escaped the fate of "looking Russian"; it would imply a disowning of her origins and her relatives who do look Russian. If she takes it as an insult—on her own behalf and on behalf of all Russian women—this would seem to call for some sort of protest or angry response in solidarity with Russian women, instead of an earnest striving to assimilate into her newer nationality.

Brodinsky's work expresses an uncompromising stand against deep-rooted mechanisms of stereotyping. In a 2006 interview, she stated, "When I started the project, I asked myself: Why am I more successful than people with a Russian accent? What would have happened if I had been blond? Am I better than someone with a name like Natasha?[1]—understanding, of course, that an accent is no longer in one's control than our physical appearance or the name that we were given at birth. I don't meet these criteria—but I still want to fight prejudices" (Rosenthal, 2006). In the book's many images, Brodinsky dons and sheds various images, uses her own body to construct an array of representations, and engages in a critical dialogue with the immigrants' stereotyping by veteran Israelis. In one image she wears heavy makeup and provocative clothing—a tight-fitting skirt and a see-through blouse—that veteran Israelis typically associate with Russian-speaking women. In another image she photographs herself as a homeless woman holding an empty bottle of vodka. Another image, in which her head is thrown backward in a way that suggests sexual climax, addresses the stereotype of Russian women as hypersexual beings and prostitutes.

Many veteran Israelis regard FSU migrants (and migrants in general) as a monolithic, uniform group and express views about their supposed collective nature and behavior that betray racist sentiments. Generalizing remarks about "Russians" are occasionally made even by academics, economists, and sociologists, whose line of work is supposed to lead them to a complex rather than a stereotyping perception of the empirical reality they study. Thus, for example, Dr. Avi Simhon, former chairman of the Finance Minister's Advisory Committee, aroused a huge public storm in 2010 by stating that "more than 450,000 migrants who have come to the country were never Jewish. Perhaps they have a grandfather who was Jewish. They've come here for economic reasons" (Basok and Zarchia, 2010). Although a substantial number of FSU migrants may indeed not be Jewish according to Halacha (which many Jews do not recognize as the sole arbitrator of Jewish identity), the preoccupation with the question of their Jewishness, along with the delegitimization of migration on socioeconomic grounds, attests primarily to the interests of the establishment, which prefers distinctly Zionist immigration.

Another example comes from sociologist Gad Yair, who spoke in an interview about the issue of gender violence among FSU migrants and stated that when he studied the subject of male violence against women, he turned to find its roots in Russian culture.

> When I wanted to understand why Russian men skewered their wives, I went to read Dostoevsky, Turgenev, Tolstoy, and saw that it is all already present there, it's all in the *Kreutzer Sonata*—it's all the same story. This is the kind of analysis I do. I don't interview the neighbours after a murder. The Russian male and Russian female, they have this [violence] in their culture. It's part of the Russian story, to drink alcohol, provoke the man, and have him finish her off in this way. (Sela, 2011: 1)

Yair's statement might serve as an example of "racism without races," known also as neo-racism, which makes no explicit mention of racial traits but instead relates to cultural differences, such as drinking and eating habits, musical preferences, or literary themes, as "natural" attributes. The phrase "racism without races," coined by Étienne Balibar (1988: 21), the French philosopher and political theoretician, denotes an elusive and labile phenomenon used by regimes to authorize and affirm racist ideologies. Without overtly using the category of race or biological attributes, this form of racism takes cultural divergences to be immutable and therefore to effectively constitute "nature" or the natural essence of a group. In this sense, sociological markers such as "Russian nature" (or "Muslim character" or "Oriental time") function as euphemisms for the term *race* (Shenhav and Yonah, 2008: 34–35).

When biological and cultural markers are confounded in this way, a society starts down the slippery slope toward racism and exclusion. Veterans impose a rigid hierarchical ranking on newcomers, marginalizing them in relation to the hegemonic culture. Frequently, the newcomers are forced to assimilate into the recipient society in ways that some experience as violent. Brodinsky's photos of distorted female figures, composed of two photos joined together by a deliberately rough seam, suggest that racial stereotyping can literally cause the body to split apart and disintegrate. In one of the works, Brodinsky is photographed as an "Olympic gymnast" whose body is made up of two parts that do not join together to make a unified, functioning whole (Figure 2).

This segmented figure ridicules the stereotype that casts all female FSU migrants as gymnasts or athletes (Brodinsky, interview by author, 2012). The dissonance and asymmetry in Brodinsky's works express her sense of a fragmented identity and a physical discomfort or disharmony, as though her body carries certain superfluous or alien organs. As she said, "My whole existence as well as the artworks in this project play on the unclear and double nature of my being an Israeli woman and a Russian woman, the emphasis lying on the dissonance that exists in the attempt to unify the different parts of my identity into a whole" (Brodinsky, interview).

In another photograph in this series, Brodinsky wears ultra-feminine clothes—a tight-fitting skirt, high heels, nylon stockings—in keeping with the stereotype of the dressing style of "Russian women." She related that this feels to her like donning a strange costume, that through this image she has been made to become someone else. The experience of one's physicality (our sense of being within our bodies) and one's outward appearance and clothing possess gender and racist aspects. Given that the body of the Other is a site of social negotiation and a tool for branding and exclusion (Lomsky-Feder and Rapoport, 2010), migrants cannot be indifferent to the matter of their visibility or nonvisibility and must always, implicitly or explicitly, face the question of revealing or hiding, exposing or concealing their foreignness. The economy of looking and issues of the gaze (both how a migrant looks at the locals and vice versa) are central to a reading of the migration phenomenon. Gaze relations thus

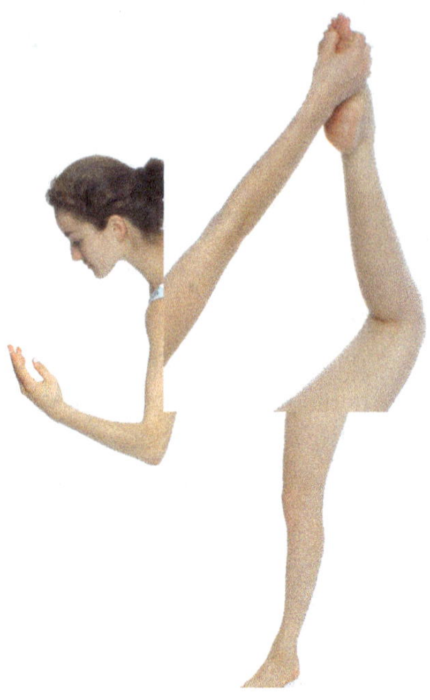

Figure 2. Tamara Brodinsky, Untitled (detail from an artist's book), 2006. Digitally manipulated color photograph.

serve as a way of forming identity: "The essence of visibility lies in identification—not just identification in the concrete sense but identification as a way of recognising the other's existence and accepting his identity" (Lomsky-Feder and Rapoport, 2010: 12).

Clothing provides migrant women with a relatively accessible and flexible space in which to manipulate their visibility. Unlike physical attributes, clothing items can quite easily be changed. Through what she wears, a woman can "cross sides" and be assimilated or else declare her difference and distinctiveness. Clothes also function as a significant interpretive tool and method of establishing out attitudes toward others. As a barometer of sorts for societal changes, clothes involve issues of identity and sexuality because they touch, both metaphorically and literally, the human body. The choice of a particular item of clothing is thus not merely a personal matter of taste but also part of the public discourse (Direktor, 2000: 5–6). In the early days of the Yishuv and after the establishment of the State of Israel, clothing served as a way of distinguishing between local and Diaspora Jews; unisex clothing and the rejection of bourgeois markers such as makeup and nylon stockings played a central role in shaping the image and body of the new Hebrew woman pioneer (Ofer, 2010: 108–9).

Although clothing did not mark Jewishness in the Soviet Union, in Israel it quite frequently gives away Russian-spreaking immigrants. Israeli veterans associate them with elegant and formal attire, shirts buttoned to the top, sandals worn with socks, and heavy makeup (Lomsky-Feder and Rapoport, 2010: 85). For their part, the immigrants navigate and construct their visibility by means of their clothing, reading and understanding local codes and clothing styles as they manifest their desire to belong or their loyalty to their country of origin and traditional codes of visibility.

Russian-speaking women testify that their clothing practices help them to establish the cross-cultural transition they undergo as immigrants, whether by freeing them up to adopt new forms of self-expression, providing an avenue for the expression of protest or self-defense, or allowing them to appear local. Edna Lomsky-Feder and Tamar Rapoport's analysis of migrant body appearance and visibility suggests that most migrant women from the FSU understand immediately upon their arrival that the clothing they had worn back home is unsuitable to the climate and physical conditions of the new country as well as inappropriate in the new society and culture (Lomsky-Feder and Rapoport, 2010: 86). One of the women they interviewed described her own ongoing process of trial and error on the way to finding her personal style in Israel, leading her at some point to revert back to wearing clothes "from there" (87).

Another of Brodinsky's photographs captures the process of identity formation involved in choosing clothing. The photograph features a young woman whose figure is split in two (composed of two photos): One part is elegantly dressed, and the other wears the simple work clothes of a housemaid, reflecting the perpetual negotiation between identity and representation (Figure 3). The artist describes this image as reflecting a dialectic move between the old and the new, which together form a hybrid identity that captures the immigrant's sense of being simultaneously European (foreign) and Israeli (local) and protests the regimenting stereotypical gaze. It also suggests that she can choose whether to deviate from or adopt the ruling norms.

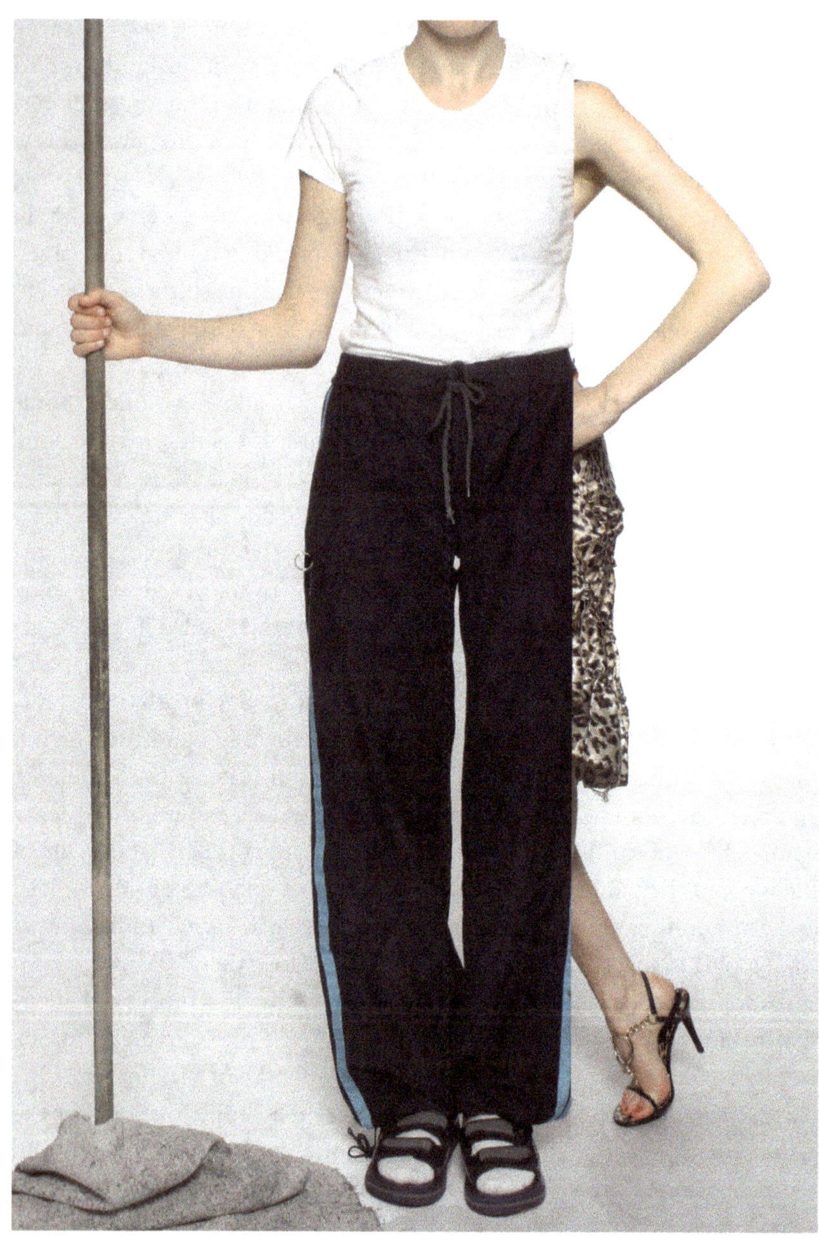

FIGURE 3. Tamara Brodinsky, Untitled (detail from an artist's book), 2006. Digitally manipulated color photograph.

GIRL-WOMAN, RUSSIAN-ISRAELI

The feelings of detachment and otherness that migration entails are reflected in the works of Anna Yam (b. 1980). Yam uses the experience of her visibility and embodiedness to express her sense of being torn between two worlds. As various art critics have observed, Yam's works express the anxiety and displacement that pervade the experience of migration (Benton and Garbuz, 2009). Yam herself notes:

> The fact that I am a migrant has an obvious influence on my artwork, just as it does on other areas of my life. Migration was a significant and traumatic event. Even now, I feel as though I am living in two parallel worlds—a Hebrew-speaking world and a Russian-speaking world. Perhaps through my art I try to preserve the dissolving Russian world in which I live, the memory of it. My family is a representative of this world, a world of migrants who are being swept away into the new culture with every day that passes. . . . On the one hand, I feel completely Israeli. I have citizenship, I know the cultural codes, the slang. . . . On the other hand, when I go to Russia, I also feel at home. I have family there, my father lives there, I have lots of memories, everything is very familiar and strange at the same time. . . . But I will never be truly inside, I'll always have an outsider's view, a different perspective. . . . The emotional dissonance, this hybridity, they are huge motivations for me. (Lael, 2008: 128–29)

The need to cope simultaneously with the forming of a new national identity and with a changing and evolving gender identity—in particular, the effects of this dual process on the nuclear family—is addressed in a Yam work from 2005 (Figure 4). In this self-portrait, taken soon after Yam's family's immigrated to Israel, the artist appears as a young girl, wearing a swimsuit.

The photograph—which was, years after, reworked by the artist—was taken on a family trip to the Dead Sea. Representing the transitional stage between girlhood and womanhood, it depicts a subject facing a double adaptation: to a new national identity and to a new female identity.[2] On her nose is a red stain—the lipsticked remnant of a kiss imprinted by her mother's lips—which serves as the symbolic seal of the female legacy passed on from generation to generation of

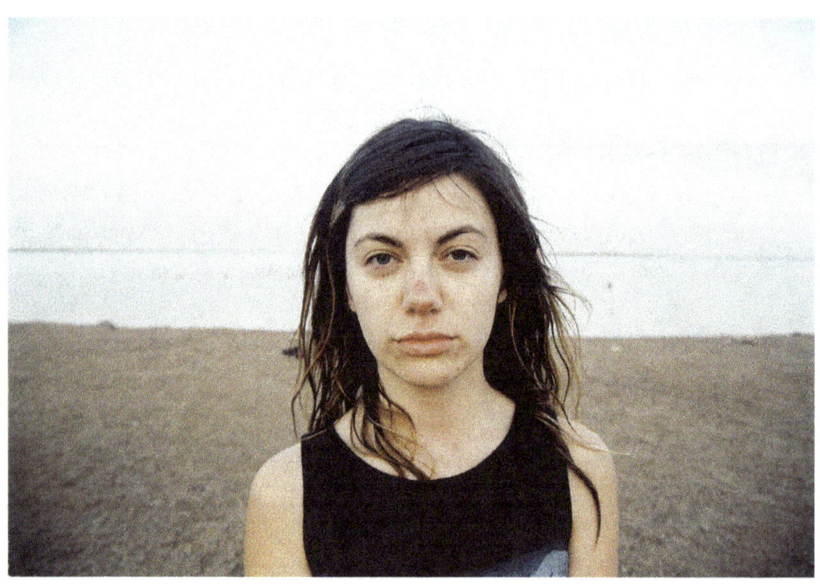

FIGURE 4. Anna Yam, Untitled, 2005. Color photo, 40 × 60 cm.

women in the family. It is the female code that has been bequeathed to her and seals her gendered fate. This work encapsulates Yam's position as a 1.5-generation immigrant. Having come to Israel at the age of 12, she experienced the crises of migration and puberty concurrently and, she says, acutely (Yam, interview by author, 2011). This formative period was influenced jointly by processes that occurred in the public, domestic, and intrapersonal spheres.

Family dynamics play a significant role in Yam's works and are often used to reflect on her migration experience. Many studies have demonstrated that migration affects the family by requiring it to cope with such complex tasks as mastering a new language, preserving memories, and adjusting to the new country. According to Vered Slonim-Nevo and Julia Mirsky (2002), how the family deals with the challenges of migration affects the way each of its members adjusts, especially adolescent family members. Slonim-Nevo and Mirsky demonstrate the existence of clear links between a quick and easy adjustment on the part of the youth and parental success in adjusting (108) and show also that youth migrants tend to view their families as facing greater difficulties than nonmigrant families (106–7).

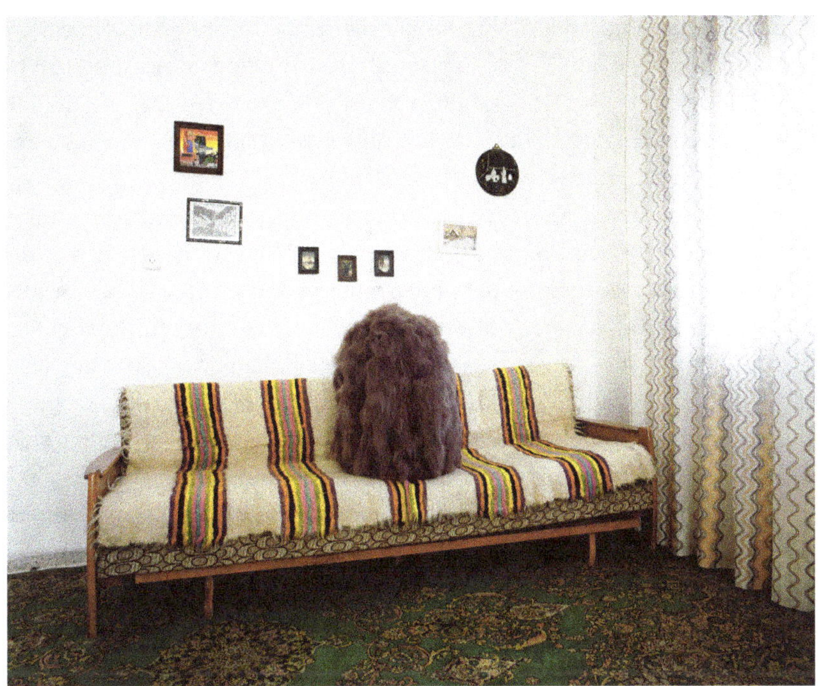

FIGURE 5. Anna Yam, Untitled, 2005. Color photo, 45 × 50 cm.

Many of Yam's works are situated in the sphere of the home and the family and are characterized by a meticulous aesthetics. Their sharp beauty captivates the eye and consoles the viewer. Yam uses odd, fetishistic domestic images that are associated with women and femininity, conveying a mixture of attraction and rejection, ease and anxiety. In a photograph from 2005, a strange swollen heap of fur rests on a lone couch in a living room, creating an unsettling atmosphere (Figure 5).

The precise nature of the hairy brown blob is hard to decipher—is it a dog? a child's toy? a hairy monster? The photograph is not immediately decodable and evokes a certain humorous or at least amused sense of discomfort. The photograph has a biographical dimension—the object placed on the couch is Yam's mother's fur coat, brought over with her from Russia. The coat marks the absence of the concrete female body. Rather than presenting the mother through her actual physical presence, the artist chooses to depict only an outward symbol—an item of clothing that once wrapped her mother's body but which is out of step with the

Israeli climate and style. "Migration frequently causes a disconnection between body and soul," Yam explains. "This situation allows a person to go on living and functioning, but in a sort of dissociated way, not unlike PTSD. The soul's experiences are not fully consistent with the body's experiences" (Yam, interview by author, 2011).

The dissociative experience produced by migration frequently creates a process of protracted coping that is never fully resolved—an "insidious trauma" in the terminology of gender researcher Effi Ziv (2012). Insidious trauma sits along the continuum that stretches between the medical discourse and critical theory; its discussion is marked by the split between these two polarized trends. The medical discourse frequently neglects the political and social dimensions (as, e.g., in the models of trauma that focus on dissociation), whereas the critical discourse focuses almost exclusively on trauma as a social phenomenon (e.g., the radical feminist discourse concerning sexual trauma). Moreover, the PTSD (post-traumatic stress disorder) recognized by the medical discourse is based on a single-event trauma that occurred in the past rather than on an ongoing trauma. Ziv suggests that we should hold both ends of the rope and create a more integrative model of trauma that incorporates mental health and politics. Yam's experience as a young girl who finds herself on the continuum between coping with the process of sexual maturation and gender identity and the trauma of migration, acclimatization, and national identity formation embodies the two poles of trauma—political and mental/physical—both of which consistently subject her to their vicissitudes.

The absence of embodied gender in Figure 5—the real body replaced by the fur coat—represents "Russian femininity" in Yam's eyes. This femininity has a long history that must be understood as it is perceived by FSU migrants. In my interview with the artist in 2011, Yam explained how the Russian concept of femininity differs from its Israeli counterpart.

> The way of life of Soviet women simultaneously enfolds within it equality between the sexes and patriarchal conservative views. Women can be found employed in jobs that are opposed to traditional ideas of femininity—construction workers, for example, who nonetheless maintain a high level of feminine elegance in their dress and outer appearance. Many women have to become a type of superwoman who proves that she can succeed in lots of areas of life. At the same time, all

sorts of regressive attitudes carry the opposite message, stressing the importance of a woman's proper aesthetic external appearance even at the expense of real achievements.

Yam encountered such views directly, as when she was deliberating whether or not to pursue a career as an architect and her grandmother advised her to keep in mind that architecture "is a very masculine profession and you'll find it difficult to stand out and succeed in it" (Yam, interview by author, 2011). Still today, Yam recounts, her grandmother often tells her to improve her appearance before she goes out, urging her to "put on some makeup, maybe put on something nicer." The message she received at home was that a woman had to look presentable in addition to being successful and taking charge of the family dynamics in the home. She must be a good daughter and a supportive wife and maintain ties with her extended family by convening family gatherings and the like. At the same time, however, she must also work hard and advance professionally.

Thus Russian culture often places women in conflicting settings that require them to internalize and realize contradictory models, such as the superwoman and the homemaker. During the Soviet era, mothers were lauded and extolled while men were not expected to take part in active parenting and were indeed excluded from the parental discourse because they were expected to realize themselves only through work and within the public sphere, where their dominance was regarded as natural and legitimate. Numerous studies—such as those conducted by Sarah Ashwin, Professor of Comparative Employment Relations at the London School of Economics—demonstrate that Soviet propaganda regarding the ideal woman was widely embraced by women, many of whom accepted that their multifaceted role was to enter the workforce, run the household, and take full charge of the child rearing (Ashwin, 2002: 119–20).

The feminist history of women in the Soviet Union differs greatly from the Western feminist narrative. Literary scholar Elana Gomel proposed a social-cultural-historical explanation of Soviet femininity. She notes that "one of the first books on Russian culture to appear in the West—Hedrick Smith's *The Russians* [1975]—memorably defined Russian women as 'liberated but not free'" (Gomel, 2006: 53). As Gomel reminds us, Russian women have always been strong and independent. As early as the eighteenth century, when English women had no legal existence independent of their husbands, aristocratic Russian women owned and ran their own estates. Russian women sought and gained access to higher education long before their European and American counterparts. They also played a prominent role in pre-Revolution radical groups. In World War I they fought on the front lines, and in World War II the 1 million Russian women who served in the army constituted the core of the frontline medical corps. The women who remained on the home front sustained the economy and "produced the ammunition that defeated Hitler" (54). Thus Russian women created for themselves "an iconic image of a secular female afflicted saint: pure, devoted, selfless, and brave" (55).

The October Revolution, according to Gomel, afforded women only a cosmetic liberation insofar as it imposed on them a dual role: Although they gained key positions in the work and professional world, they were also required to continue devoting their time to traditional feminine tasks, so that "the image of the Soviet woman was a paradoxical one . . . she was supposed to be simultaneously strong and slim, modest and sexy, maternal and beguiling" (Gomel, 2006: 57). Gomel argues that this reality lies behind the high rates of divorce and single motherhood in Russia and also accounts for the fact that few women could afford to have more than one child.[3] "With the collapse of the Soviet Union, the impossible ideal of Soviet femininity also disappeared, leaving behind it two conflicting messages: the woman had to take care of herself and the woman had to sustain traditional conduct and be feminine" (58). It is the legacy of this already complex and conflicting definition of gender identity that FSU migrant women brought with them to Israel, where the encounter with a new social, cultural, and political reality further compounded gender identity questions (Remennick, 1999: 165–67).

RACIST SEXISM

One of the most complex gender issues facing Russian-speaking migrant women in Israel is the stereotype of the Russian prostitute. An example of the women artists' preoccupation with this persistent stereotype is found in *A Matter of Approach*, a video series created by Rufina Muraviova Lin (b. 1977) and shown at the 2012 "Proofs" exhibition at Sapir College (Figure 6). The video series presents a sequence of random encounters documented by the artist with a hidden camera over the course of four

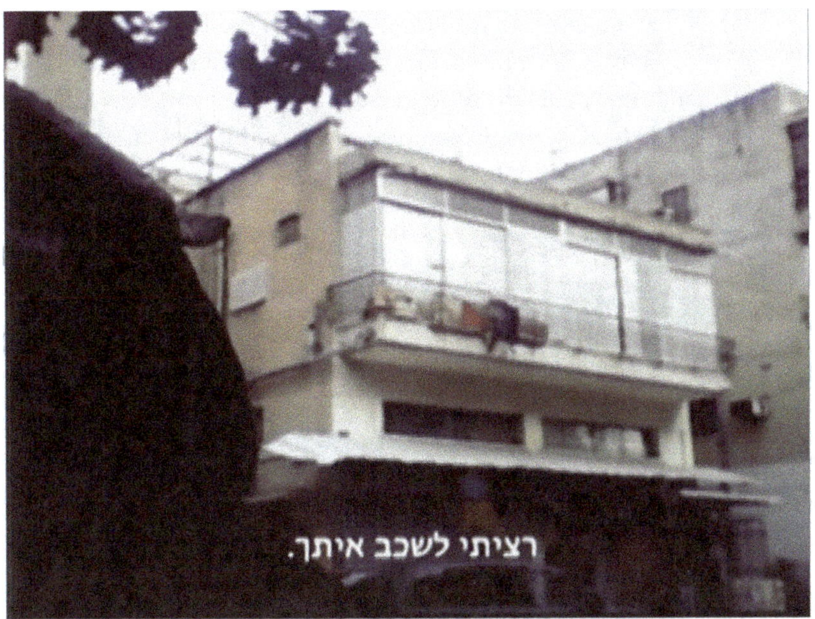

Figure 6. Rufina Muraviova Lin, *A Matter of Approach*, 2011. Still from a video (a film supported by the CCA/Israeli Fund for Video Art and Experimental Cinema, Tel Aviv).

years. As part of the project, Muraviova Lin visited cities across Israel and documented men who approached her with various proposals ranging from ostensible companionship to direct solicitations of sex for money. Muraviova Lin's tiny camera was concealed in a necklace. She herself does not appear in the videos; only her voice is recorded.

In one scene Muraviova Lin is approached by a helmeted man on a Vespa who begins talking to her. He asks her to step aside with him, and she refuses. He then parks the Vespa on the pavement, walks up to her, introduces himself by name, and tries again to strike up a conversation. Eventually he offers her money and asks her to go home with him; she declines. The surrealism of this scene is enhanced by the appearance in the background of a gaunt woman, probably homeless, looking into an industrial waste bin for food, her entire upper body buried in the bin and invisible. The following exchange is a transcription of part of the dialogue between the artist and the biker, as heard on the soundtrack of the video.

Man: What a nice smile you've got! Beautiful eyes! . . . I thought . . . in Tel Aviv . . . I could find a girl. To sleep together. At night. I'm a handsome man. You're good looking, too. A baby. There'll be a baby. Pretty. Green. Green eyes. [Takes off his helmet.]
Rufina Muraviova Lin: Is that it?
Man: I wanted to sleep with you.
RML: Anything else?
Man: Do you want to go get a room in a hotel?
RML: No.
Man: I'll get a room in a hotel. [Draws money out of his pocket, then replaces it.] I've got a lot more.
RML: Great. And . . . ?
Man: Together, you and me. We'll eat a meal there. Here, in Tel Aviv. We'll rent a room.
RML: I don't want to.
Man: Come here, closer.
RML: I don't want to.
Man: Two hours. I'll give you money, too.
Artist: Really?!
Man: I swear. How much do you want?
RML: I don't want.
Man: Want 150 NIS?
RML: No.
Man: You'll have money.
RML: I have money.
Man: Come on. So you'll have more.

The video series raises questions about the ways in which Israeli men behave when they encounter FSU women immigrants, as reflected through the eyes of a young immigrant woman. "I often use a hidden camera," Muraviova Lin recounts. "Through the video camera I can photograph strange and sometimes dangerous situations that I could not document with an ordinary camera, especially in light of the fact that, in most cases, I myself am involved in the situations" (Muraviova Lin, personal correspondence, 2012). In my interview with the artist in 2012, she stated that the idea of using a hidden camera for her art was born out of necessity—videotaping the harassment she experienced furnished her with proof in case she opted to turn to the police.

As Muraviova Lin notes, the dynamics depicted in the video works derive directly from her identity as a FSU woman migrant: "Because I am a Russian woman in the State of Israel, this [harassment] is definitely a subject that I deal with. . . . Most of my personal artistic 'research' is about the relationship between men and women, a complex issue. In order to examine it, I use the hidden camera as an aid. Personally, I've always been the object of male attention because I fit the Russian 'type'—I'm blond and pretty" (Muraviova Lin, interview by author, 2012).

Through her reflexive engagement with this dynamic, Muraviova Lin has come to regard herself not as a helpless victim but rather as an active agent who initiates and creates art that is critical of her circumstances. "For many years, I really found it hard to deal with the male Israeli attitude toward women. But from the moment I started doing this kind of art, it gave me power to deal with the situation and shape it. A good-looking blond Russian woman—that's a difficulty. But a good-looking, blond Russian woman armed with a hidden camera—that's power!" (Muraviova Lin, interview by author, 2012).

The hidden camera, then, is at once a practical and an artistic tool, with Muraviova Lin adopting the role of an investigative journalist, as it were, and using the visual language of TV shows and reports that expose conmen. She sets her gaze on offensive men, positioning them as the object of a personal as much as a general cultural criticism. The clips deconstruct the gaze relations by allowing the artists to "look at the way in which they look at me" (Muraviova Lin, interview by author, 2012).

As Lomsky-Feder and Rapoport observed in their study of gaze relation between immigrants and locals, the dynamics described by Muraviova Lin constitute a demand to obtain "identification that is recognition of the existence of the other and acceptance of his identity" (2010: 12). The hidden-camera videos provide a formal and literal transcript of situations of this kind of visibility and mutual gazing. Muraviova Lin's gaze is concealed but critical, simultaneously present and absent. As she observes, the gaze relations in her works seek to break down the power relations: "Ultimately, everything in life is a game of roles, who exploits whom, what each side wants from the other side. To my mind, a man's relation to a 'non-artist' woman is not the same as to a woman who is an artist. If I take a camera and set out to film 'men,' I have a very specific goal" (Muraviova Lin, personal correspondence, 2012). Muraviova Lin's aim is thus to use her art to prompt a discourse concerning this painful, silenced subject.

According to a recent survey, Russian-speaking woman living in Israel report experiencing harassment at much higher rates than the female population at large. In the *Women's Security Index Report* survey—a joint publication by a coalition of six feminist organizations (Kayan, Isha Le–Isha-Haifa Feminist Center, the Coalition of Women for Peace, Women Against Violence, Aswat, and New Profile) published in 2012—researchers sought to create a security index that would test the level of safety experienced by women from various social groups in Israel. The broad-based survey found that 32% of Russian-speaking women reported feeling humiliated or attacked (as opposed to 14% of women from among the general Jewish female populace who gave similar reports). Of the Russian-speaking women, 38% reported having been sexually assaulted by a man whom they did not know, compared with 16% among the general female Jewish population (Istuchina and Zamir, 2012: 6).

Feminist activist Inna Michaeli describes the close link between the woman migrant's body and harassment or sexual violence.

> Migration is inscribed on the body. On the contours of the face, in the sounds of the voice. In the accent. When I arrived in Israel with the mass wave of immigration from the FSU at the beginning of the 1990s, I was nine years old. I was familiar with the cultural link between Russian women and prostitution long before I learned about the sexual harassment of Russian women unaware of their rights. . . . As a migrant, it was as though my body was declaring 'I'm not from here.' My body and I, we have a common past—before Israel. We come from another place. So the dominance of this place over us is limited. This foreignness serves me as a defence and creates a safe distance from the significations attributed to me, to my body, to my sexuality. . . . [In Israel] the image of my body is shaped and constructed from within a reality in which the body of a "Russian woman" embodies easy sexual access. (Michaeli, 2011: 38)

As Michaeli indicates, in Israel, the link between the Russian-speaking woman's body and the gross sexual stereotyping attached to it is perceived as inextricable, with many FSU migrant women being called Russian whores (Golden, 2003). As Lomsky-Feder and Rapoport argue, the objectification and stereotyping pave the way for sexual harassment: "The aim of the objectifying gaze and the insults designed to hurt is to devalue Russian women by cheapening their bodies. Marking a body as immoral legitimizes the harassment and leads to a physical and verbal infringement of its boundaries" (Lomsky-Feder and Rapoport, 2010: 79).

The construction and perpetuation of stereotypes about FSU migrant women as prostitutes is strikingly evident in Israeli media in general and in the printed press in particular, as media scholar Dafna Lemish's research demonstrates. The findings of Lemish's quantitative study, conducted in 2000, indicate that most media references to FSU immigrant women related to prostitution, alongside two other categories: their being "different and foreign" and their being "exceptionally successful" (Lemish, 2000: 341–43). Designed to designate their bodies as "other," the coupling of the epithet "Russian whore" with the migrant women in the context of the Jewish Israeli collective thus transforms the "Russian" female body into an active site for the marking of national boundaries (Golden, 2003).

RACISM AND SEX TRAFFICKING

The sexual stereotyping of FSU migrant women in Israel sometimes takes a particularly gross and blatant form of exploitation. Sex trafficking is addressed in the works of artist Anna Kuntsman Rozenberg (b. 1981). In 2010 she created *Catherine the Great*, an animated short film (4:57 minutes) that addresses the subject of FSU women who are victims of the global prostitution industry and were transported into Israel for that purpose. The piece uses several animation techniques, including paper cutouts with drawn elements (Figure 7). The decorative style is derived from the traditional Russian wood-painting handicraft style known as *khokhloma*, thereby creating a link between Kunstsman Rozenberg's work and traditional feminine crafts in general (such as embroidery, decoration, and carpet weaving).

The film was prompted by Kuntsman Rozenberg's personal experience with the stigmatization of Russian-speaking women in Israel as hypersexual in general and prostitutes in particular.[4] *Catherine the Great* reveals the stories of women who have fallen victim to sex traffickers and are forced to become prostitutes. In preparing the work, Kuntsman Rozenberg researched

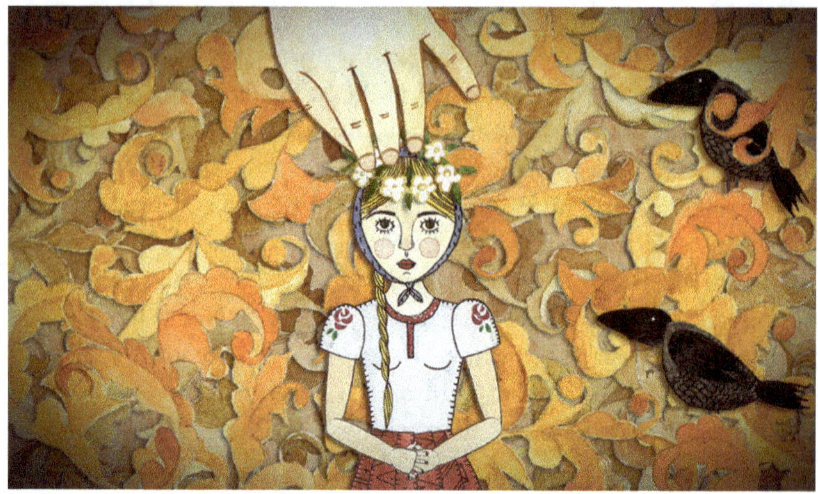

FIGURE 7. Anna Kuntsman Rozenberg, *Catherine the Great*, 2010. Detail from an animated film.

the subject, ultimately deciding to focus on Ilana Hammerman's book *In Foreign Parts: Trafficking Women in Israel* (2004). The film is a first-person narration of the life of a young woman from Moldova who answers an advertisement for an au pair job and finds herself smuggled into Israel by way of Egypt and forced to work as a prostitute. The narrator for the protagonist, whose voice is heavily accented, is actress Alena Yiv, who plays the lead in an Israeli television show about sex trafficking (*Blue Natalie*). Kuntsman Rozenberg's film describes the woman's emotional experience, her mental breakdown, and her eventual dissociation ("It's not I who am lying here, it's another girl.") According to Kuntsman Rozenberg, she chose animation as the medium through which to tell a story that society does not want to hear as a way of circumventing the numbness that afflicts audiences when they are confronted with difficult themes and as a way of allowing the audience to identify with the female figure.

Catherine the Great makes metaphorical use of the painful subject of sex trafficking to address the larger theme that interests Kuntsman Rozenberg: the relationship between FSU migrant women and veteran Israelis. Precisely because the work deals with non-Jewish women who did not make aliyah for ideological reasons and have no part in the Zionist narrative, it is able to convey the artist's own experience of being constantly suspected by Israeli veterans of being a non-Jewish Russian prostitute. The work protests the stereotyping that the artist herself and other migrant women experience in Israeli society. Kuntsman Rozenberg, who is indeed Jewish, came to Israel at a young age and regards herself as Israeli. Nonetheless—and despite her extended military service as an officer in the IDF, an important marker of belonging for Israelis—she has frequently been discriminated against by the host society and suffers from abusive comments related to her origin.

Anthropologist Deborah Golden notes that the potential lure to Jewish men posed by the arrival of hundreds of thousands of Russian women whose Jewishness is widely doubted has become the source of a national existential fear since the massive wave of immigration of the 1990s. These women, she observes, are perceived as threatening the Jewish collective purity and Israel's ethnonational identity because their offspring would also be considered non-Jews according to Jewish law, diluting Jewish men's pure blood (Jewish identity being matrilineal) (Golden, 2003: 92–93). Whereas in the FSU, Jewish women were considered "sexually modest and moral," in Israel their bodies have become branded with a stigma that "attributes an impurity to them that must be banished beyond the boundaries of Jewish-Israeli nationality" (Lomsky-Feder and Rapoport, 2010: 79).

Unfortunately, the stigma of the Russian prostitute has some basis in reality, both in Israel and across the globe. In an article titled "The 'Natasha' Trade: Transnational Sex Trafficking," Donna Hughes remarks:

> Countries with large sex industries create the demand for women; countries where traffickers recruit women provide the supply. For decades, the primary sending countries were in Asia. But the collapse of the Soviet Union opened up a pool of millions of women from which traffickers can recruit. Former Soviet republics such as Belarus, Latvia, Moldova, Russia, and Ukraine have become major suppliers of women to sex industries all over the world. In the sex industry today, the most popular and valuable women are from Russia and the Ukraine. (Hughes, 2011: 9)

The international prostitution industry, or what is known as sex trafficking, is a particularly cruel and abominable phenomenon. The biopower exerted against women forced into it in today's increasingly globalized world is so sophisticated and powerful that it is virtually unstoppable. This biopower not only creates a class of excluded women but also establishes a euphemized construct of these women in the eyes of the "customers," who use them as objects, denying their status as real subjects and human beings. As objects and sex machines, these women are stripped of their humanity. All this takes place within the global capitalist system that relates to human sexual needs in economic terms and ships women all over the world in order to meet the demand. Within the broad spectrum of labor migration, this type of forced prostitution, accompanied typically by kidnapping and repeated rape, constitutes a most brutal extreme.[5]

EMPLOYMENT

Many FSU migrant women began their occupational paths in Israel in what are typically called unskilled jobs—cashiers, cleaners, caregivers, security guards (Steir and Levanon, 2003). Even though many ex-Soviet migrants, and the younger generation in particular, have gradually mastered the language and other tools required to navigate the Israeli job market and have successfully moved into other professions, these unskilled trades have become associated with Russian-speaking women. This linkage has created a stereotypical cultural construct, most memorably embodied in the popular figure of Luba, a fictional character who is regularly featured on the satirical Israeli show *Eretz Nehederet* (A Wonderful Land) and who is a parody of a female Russian supermarket cashier.

In 2005 the artist Ania Krupiakov (b. 1983) photographed a series of FSU migrant women working as cleaners through a subcontracting company. The women were all employed under the kind of exploitative conditions to which migrants are particularly vulnerable, including delayed payment of wages, no payment for travel time (especially prevalent in the caregiving industry), subminimum hourly wages (principally in part-time jobs), a minimal pension that leads them into poverty when they retire, and a general and frequent exploitation of the migrants' lack of awareness of their rights or else the vagueness of the rights themselves (Nisim and Benjamin, 2010). Krupiakov chose to turn her camera on the gender aspects of poverty employment, photographing migrant women and exhibiting a particular sensitivity to discrimination on the basis of age (ageism). In this series of portraits, the cleaning women are photographed at work—in malls, offices, and cinemas (Figures 8 and 9).

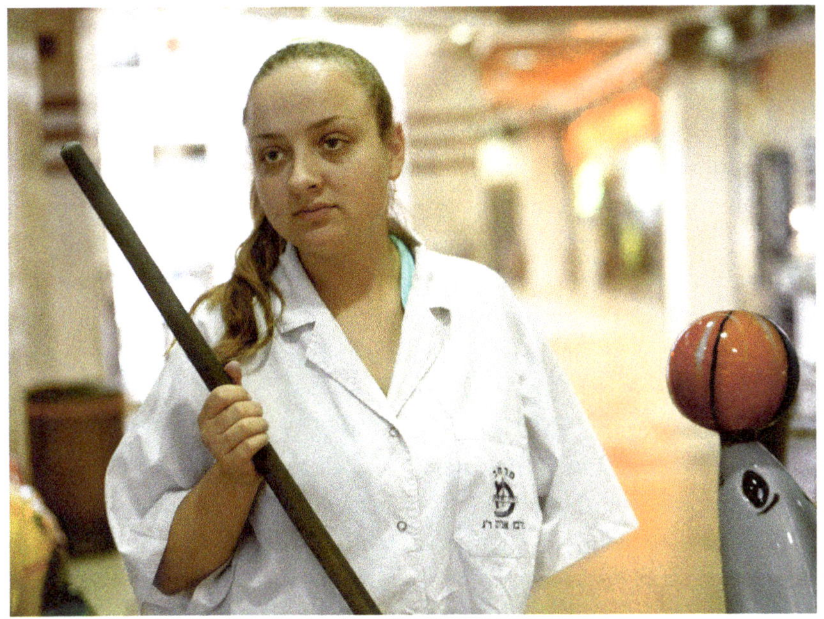

Figure 8. Ania Krupiakov, Untitled, 2005. Color photograph.

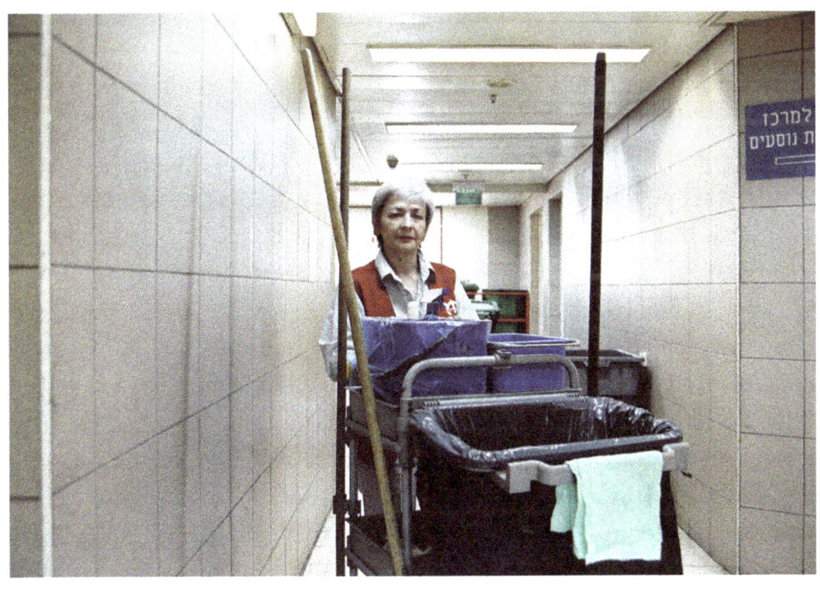

Figure 9. Ania Krupiakov, Untitled, 2005. Color photograph.

In Figure 8 the camera captures a young woman holding a broom and wearing the uniform of the cleaning company that employs her. Her gaze is unfocused, turned away from the camera, as though embodying the boredom and frustration of the job's monotonous, long hours. In the background, the shopping mall—symbol of the ever-growing neoliberal economies—dissolves out of focus. Figure 9 features a gray-haired woman pushing a trolley stocked with cleaning materials and a large rubbish bin. Her expression is forlorn, perhaps reflecting the need to work at a job that does not at all suit her professional qualifications and life experience. She stands in a long, sterile corridor that stretches sharply into the distance, threatening to draw her into its vacuum.

Krupiakov attests that the preparatory meetings she held with the women before photographing them were charged and difficult (Krupiakov, interview by author, 2012). Particularly meaningful was her meeting with one of the elderly women, who assumed a motherly attitude toward Krupiakov, saying that she was like her daughter, that she felt close to her, and urging Krupiakov to persist in gaining a higher education so that she could succeed in Israel. The meeting was long and intense, with the woman telling her story in tears and Krupiakov herself weeping in empathy on several occasions. The woman holds a master's degree in chemistry and immigrated relatively late in life, after a flourishing career. In Israel, however, she had to take a job as a cleaner through a subcontracting company, working with no job security.

The predicament and sentiments of FSU migrant workers reduced to cleaning and similar minimum-wage jobs have been addressed in academic studies, which paint a complex picture (Remennick, 1999: 170–72). Orly Benjamin and colleagues' sociological study (2010) indicates that most FSU migrant women working as cleaners do not report feeling ashamed of their work—perhaps because they view it as an inevitable and temporary stage in the process of their adjustment to the new country and therefore not a defining component of their professional identity. They do report great difficulty, however, with a different aspect of their work, namely, the interactions with co-workers (primarily nonmigrant). The feelings of humiliation reported, for example, by hospital cleaners (who constituted the case study of this research) derive not from a negative or critical attitude of family or community members but rather from being regularly ignored by the medical staff and being denied even the most basic level of courtesy. This feeling is accompanied by one of deep frustration in the face of what amounts to a dehumanizing attitude on the part of their superiors, manifested, for example, in the monitoring of their every move, in not considering them even minimally dependable, or imposing on them capricious tasks (Benjamin et al., 2010: 343, 350).

The centrality of the career and employment world to the people's identity formation under the Soviet regime has recently motivated gender scholars to examine gender issues linked to employment in the Eastern bloc after its collapse. Numerous studies address this issue, especially as it relates to the transitional period following the disintegration of the Soviet Union. Many gender scholars assumed that after the collapse of communism, women would return more or less en masse to their traditional domestic roles, abandoning the professional world they had been forced to enter by communist ideology and national struggles (Funk and Mueller, 1993; Pilkington 1992). Because the women's entry into the workforce was not voluntary, these scholars assumed that the emancipatory logic of the Western world would lead them to return to the home and to the traditional gender roles to which they had been accustomed before the communist revolution (Lissyutkina, 1993: 274).

This did not happen. After the fall of communism, women did not return to their traditional gender roles, but nor did they succeed in progressing toward a more egalitarian reality (Ashwin, 2002: 117). According to Ashwin, the explanation lies in the nature of Russian culture. During the Soviet era, gender roles followed the needs of the state above all else and were largely determined by these needs. In exchange for fulfilling the roles that it demanded of them, the state guaranteed women its protection and funding of a wide range of educational frameworks. The preeminent role of women during this period was that of the working woman–mother, with women joining the workforce and producing the next generation of workers by cultivating the home, children, and family. Being the central pillar of Soviet civic identity, work became a central site of social integration in Soviet society (119). Statistics from the end of the communist era demonstrate that the rate of female participation in the workforce approached the biological maximum (119).

The difficulties that FSU migrants in Israel encounter in finding employment in their original occupations are various and include limited job opportunities in the peripheries and a difficulty in mastering the language

(Philippov, 2010: 4–5). The stereotype embodied by the character of Luba the supermarket cashier on the one hand and the Soviet culture of dignity and a self-image based largely on the work life on the other have led to a crisis among many ex-Soviet migrants, particularly older women.

A study of FSU migrants published in 2010 examined the difficulties in absorption and adjustment encountered by women on their arrival in Israel (Mor, 2010). Many of the participants worked in low-paying jobs, such as washing dishes at event halls or cleaning homes and offices. For these migrants, many of whom hold academic degrees, the step down in employment status caused both economic and emotional stress. Many reported being exploited at work, experiencing severe difficulties in covering their rent, traveling by foot rather than by public transport, trying to find work in restaurants in order to get free meals, experiencing conflicts in their families as a result of economic pressures, and numerous other experiences of privation that affected their quality of life.

The coping mechanisms of women who find themselves in such circumstances have been described by sociologist Beverley Skeggs as emotional politics, meaning that they have sophisticated strategies of identity management and coping mechanisms to maintain their self-esteem (Skeggs, 1997). Using this concept, Benjamin and colleagues analyzed the emotional politics that emerged from women's responses to exclusion in the socially degrading field of cleaning among Mizrahi, ex-Soviet, and Israeli-Palestinian women. Their study shows that "these women challenge oppressive social structures by cultivating a sense of pride, dignity, and belonging, together with the consolidation of a community" (Benjamin et al., 2010: 337). An example of such a communal response is the Workers Committee established by some 200 cleaners at Ben-Gurion University of the Negev, the first cleaning women's organization in Israel. Valentina Lichotinsky, a member of the Workers Committee, says:

> It was not political pretensions that drove the establishment of this organization but a simple goal: the will to survive. We won many small victories in our struggle, including a guarantee of continued employment when moving from one contractor to another; forcing the University to turn on the air conditioning system especially for us in the early morning hours, when we start working; success in signing a collective work agreement; and more.... [These are] "modest" tar-

gets that were achieved through huge efforts—and they all have one goal: the right to visibility. Only a "transparent" worker doesn't get to have air conditioning in the heat of Beersheba. A struggle of this kind cannot succeed without public visibility. We were helped by several journalists in various media platforms. (Lichotinsky, 2012)

WHO IS A JEW?

One of the most difficult and distressing issues facing many FSU migrants in Israel concerns the question of their Jewishness (Sweifach, 2005). The matter bears directly on questions of citizenship, the right to receive various government funds, the migrants' sense of community and belonging, and many additional aspects. Yasna Goldshmidt (b. 1985) addresses the question of who is a Jew through a gender perspective in her video work *He Who Has Made Me a Non-Jewess* (5:20 minutes), which recounts her personal biography through the prism of her Jewish identity and gives voice to her feelings of exclusion from Israeli society (Figure 10).

As mentioned, Israel gives automatic citizenship based on ethnoreligious principles (jus sanguinis, right of blood) rather than on place of birth (jus soli, right of the soil) and welcomes Jewish immigrants in accordance with the Declaration of Independence and the Law of Return,

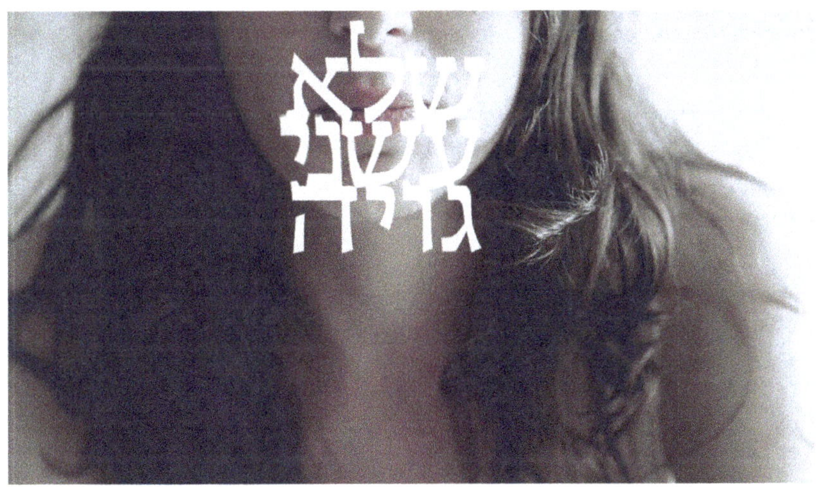

Figure 10. Yasna Goldshmidt, *He Who Has Made Me a Non-Jewess*, 2011. Still from a video.

enacted in 1950 and amended in 1970. The Law of Return, which has the status of a Basic Law, states that a Jew has the natural right to return to his or her historic homeland and that every Jew and the members of his or her family who immigrate to Israel will automatically receive citizenship (Shuval and Leshem, 1998). To immigrate and gain citizenship, immigrants must provide documents proving their Jewish status but do not need to prove a social or emotional connection with the Jewish people or any familiarity with the Jewish tradition (Ben-Raphael, 2001). Goldshmidt was born in Leningrad and later moved with her family to Moldova. Her father is Jewish; her mother is not. Although Jewish law does not consider her a Jew, the Law of Return nonetheless allows her to make aliyah. She first came to Israel as a high school student on a Birthright trip, a project designed to strengthen the connection of young Jews with Israel and their Jewish identity.[6] She subsequently immigrated on her own, without her family, as part of the Selah project—its name a Hebrew acronym for the phrase "students before their parents."[7]

In the video Goldshmidt tells her life story in the format of an interview, without looking directly at the camera. The film also incorporates old movie segments of her family and her life in Moldova, such as her studies in a Jewish elementary school and events in the life of the Jewish community of Kishinev, such as the building of a sukkah during Sukkot or celebrating Tu B'Shevat tree planting. The artist later describes her farewell to her homeland and her flight to Israel, the sorrow of parting, and the joys of her new life in Israel. In a key segment of the video she recounts how she used to pray during her conversion course in Israel: "Blessed be You, O Lord our God, king of the world, who has not made me a non-Jewess."[8] She describes waking one morning to the realization that this sentence encapsulates her liminal status. Was it appropriate for her to say it or not? While not halachically Jewish, she was not a full-blown Gentile either. The film ends with the statement, "My name is Yasna Goldshmidt and I am 25 years old. I emigrated from Kishinev, Moldova. I was born in Leningrad, Russia. I live here alone." This is a laconic but direct and unambiguous description of her present multilayered identity and her predicament in Israel. She is not regarded as Jewish by the state authorities, but she lives in the country and sees her future in Israel.

Unlike the clear-cut rabbinic laws regarding Jewish identity, the self-definition of FSU migrants is relative and multilayered. In a qualitative study,

Vered Mor conducted in-depth interviews with FSU migrant women and found that most of those whose Jewishness was questioned by the rabbinate based their own definition of their religious identity on personal interpretation and feelings rather than on the precise stipulations of Halacha. "Most of the women thought that a 'Jew' was someone who had at least one Jewish parent, emphasizing that they believed that it does not matter whether the Jewish parent was the father or the mother. None of the respondents mentioned familiarity with Jewish culture or observance of tradition as a prerequisite for belonging to the Jewish people" (Mor, 2010: 79).

Personal interpretation and a range of contradictory feelings about her Jewish identity are an integral part of Yasna Goldshmidt's experience. From a young age she has experienced her identity as out of synch with her environment, feeling herself to be too Jewish in Russia and not Jewish enough in Israel. She reports that the task she took upon herself in setting out to make *He Who Has Made Me a Non-Jewess*, which involved deep self-exploration and an attempt to measure or assess her Jewishness and belonging to the Jewish people, proved to be emotionally taxing. From the start, the creative process aroused a great ambivalence within her, nearly causing her to abandon the project. Her reluctance to engage in the subject, she says, stemmed from her fear that the process would reopen old wounds (Goldshmidt, interview by author, 2012).

This heightened sensitivity to questions of identity accompanies Goldshmidt in her daily life and rears its head in unexpected places. Thus, for example, when she was working as a salesperson in a clothes shop, she would ask customers to show some form of ID with their credit card, and she found that her eyes gravitated immediately to the line in the Israeli ID card that notes the holder's ethnic affiliation—a category that effectively delineates religious affiliation.

> The truth is that I never looked at the photo or identified the person visually when I looked at their identification card, my eyes always went to the category of religious identity. . . . You know, I'll never be able to marry or be buried here because I did not complete the conversion course. I really don't know what will happen with that. Yes, it's offensive. If that's how things are, why does the Jewish Agency bother to bring us here—if in the end they disown us?! (Goldshmidt, interview by author, 2012)

Goldshmidt also highlights the gender aspect of this sensitive subject: "For men whose Jewishness is doubted, this is also not easy. Yet the issue of Judaism is less critical for them than it is for women. They can marry a Jewish woman and their children will thus be Jewish, ensuring their future. As a woman, I can't guarantee the future status of my children" (Goldshmidt, interview by author, 2012).

Most scholars concur that about one-third of the FSU migrants who have come to Israel under the Law of Return since the 1990s are not halachically Jewish. The attitudes toward them in Israeli society—on the part of the veteran civic population and various religious authorities—vary greatly, ranging from complete rejection through various degrees of reservation and indifference to total acceptance (Remennick, 2007; Smooha, 2008). Israeli law, which restricts the rights of many such citizens to marry in the country (Hacker, 2012), effectively renders them second-class citizens, claims Alex Tantzer, a social activist who works with FSU migrants (Tantzer, 2012: 16). According to the Israeli Central Bureau of Statistics, between 1990—the first year of the great wave of FSU migration—and 2000, the number of Israelis registered as married in Cyprus rose by nearly twelve-fold (from 270 in 1990 to 3,170 in 2000).

As the decade progressed, the number of Israeli citizens turning to overseas marriage declined, a fact explained by legal changes, regulations regarding marital relationships, and most prominently the rise in the number of couples choosing to live together without marrying. Tantzer describes the difficulties encountered by Israelis born in the FSU who are defined as non-Jewish or whose Jewishness is questioned when they seek to marry: They undergo a thorough background check by the rabbinate, which holds the mandate to marital registration, are only allowed to marry a non-Jew, like them, or else, if they marry a Jew, must do so outside the country: "These people who marry abroad live in the country as Israeli citizens for all intents and purposes. They serve in the army, pay taxes, fulfill all the other duties imposed on citizens by the State—and yet the State makes them feel as though they are second-class citizens and makes no attempt to determine their rights before the law" (Tantzer, 2012: 16).

Goldshmidt's work encapsulates this painful predicament of many Russian speakers in Israel. Toward the end of her film, she states, "I want to be buried here. I want to marry here. I want children. The main thing that offends me in this whole business is the thought of my grandparents, of blessed memory, who write in their biographies that their parents were killed in concentration camps or on the way there—and I see myself with them."

CULTURAL BRANDING

Contra the veteran Israeli gaze, which automatically places all ex-Soviet migrants into a single ethnoreligious category, the FSU migration is far from homogeneous. After the disintegration of the Soviet Union, the huge conglomerate split into fifteen republics belonging to Asia and Europe. But even when the Soviet Union was one country, great differences existed between the residents of its Asian and European regions—differences of geography and climate, of local culture and religion. Of the FSU migrants who arrived between 1990 and 1995, 79% came from the European republics and 21% from the Asian republics (Sikron and Leshem, 1998: 19).

The art produced by immigrants from the Asian republics typically reflects a culture that is a mixture of pan-Soviet and local elements. Artist Rimma Arslanov (b. 1978) is a multimedia artist whose work is influenced by many sources and styles. One of her sculptures, *Mashrabiya*, is a large piece (60 × 1,230 × 120 cm) that imitates the architectonic element of a lattice (Figure 11). The piece is constructed out of sheets of wood covered by layers of foam and soft, gray-silver synthetic fur. The work relates both to the original Arab *mashrabiya* and to the artist's Uzbeki-Russian roots in a kind of contemporary Israeli blend of Western and Middle Eastern elements. Arslanov enlarges the object beyond its normal proportions and clothes it with a softness that is full of humor and seemingly breathes life into it. The oversized sculpture arouses curiosity and surprises the viewer, also serving as a seductive object that seems to call out to be touched and caressed (Peleg-Rotem, 2011).

"*Mashrabiya* is a major element in my work," says Arslanov. "From afar, the fur-covered *mashrabiya* gives the impression of being firm, as if made of concrete, but when you get closer, you see that it's covered with gray fur. It's something hard covered with something soft. You have to remember that fur also has a sexual, alluring connotation" (Arslanov, interview by author, 2012). *Mashrabiya* is a fascinating object because of the liminality of its positioning: It is at once an integral part of an external wall and also an

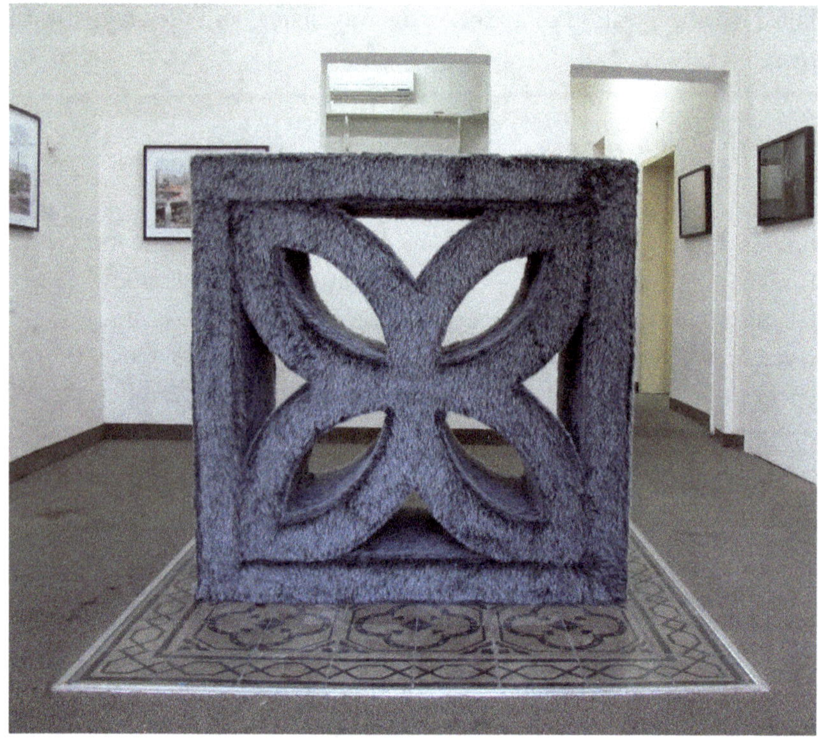

Figure 11. Rimma Arslanov, *Mashrabiya*, 2011, Wood, cloth, and synthetic fur.

interruption in the wall's flow, serving as a window that opens up space in the architectonic expanse. It is not simply a functional solution that allows cool air to flow into the house in hot climates but also part of a culture, primarily Islamic, in which women remain within the domestic space, from where they peer outside without themselves being seen.

In an interview with Arslanov, the artist explained the inspiration for her work.

> The sources of my work come first of all from the place where I am from, Uzbekistan. All the elements and ornaments in my work come from the carpets, the culture, and from what I learned in my artistic education there. For example, we had a course in ornamentation. Nonetheless, my deliberate use of ornamentation started only in

> Israel, after my studies at the Avni Institute of Art, when I began painting myself against a background of Uzbeki carpets. Gradually, the ornaments turned into something else, they dissolved, changed, became black or gray rather than colorful, they underwent a transformation. (Armon Azoulay, 2012: 5)

Throughout the history of Western art, crafts and decorative arts have been regarded as the domain of women, an inferior form of art distinguished from the "real" art produced by men. This tendency is particularly evident in the modern period, which has rejected pattern and decoration artifacts and classified them as inferior (Dekel, 2013: 58–65). Around the mid-twentieth century, women artists with a feminist agenda began incorporating decorative elements regarded as crafts, especially such elements from non-European sources, in a deliberate protest against the condescending attitude of Western hegemonic art toward this art form. Works of this type sought to reveal the power relations behind the contemporary discourse regarding the canon of art—a discourse that defines decoration as feminine, as Other, and far inferior to the "male" abstract, minimalistic, and conceptual art that ruled at that time (Broude, 1994: 208).

Another work by Arslanov, *Tank Driver*, features an armored soldier constructed out of cement and sand whose uniform and helmeted head are wrapped in an elaborate decorative pattern (Figure 12). The image of the tank driver is one of a long series of images of soldiers created by Arslanov. She says of this theme, "The soldiers are a subject that I have dealt with for more than three years in my art. These are small toy soldiers, looking like little phalluses, most of them bent slightly forward. They're rather ridiculous. I have some sort of resistance and even repulsion toward the violence that militarist masculinity endorses and promotes. It's something that really riles me" (Arslanov, interview by author, 2012).

Drawing on her own childhood memories, Arslanov reconstructs war toys, typically considered the domain of boys, that she often used to play with. She returns repeatedly to the figure of a green toy soldier, her favorite toy as a child. Her "wrapping" of the soldier, a symbol of aggression, with beautiful ornamentation, associated with femininity, can be interpreted as a subversive act that sets itself against and seeks to undermine

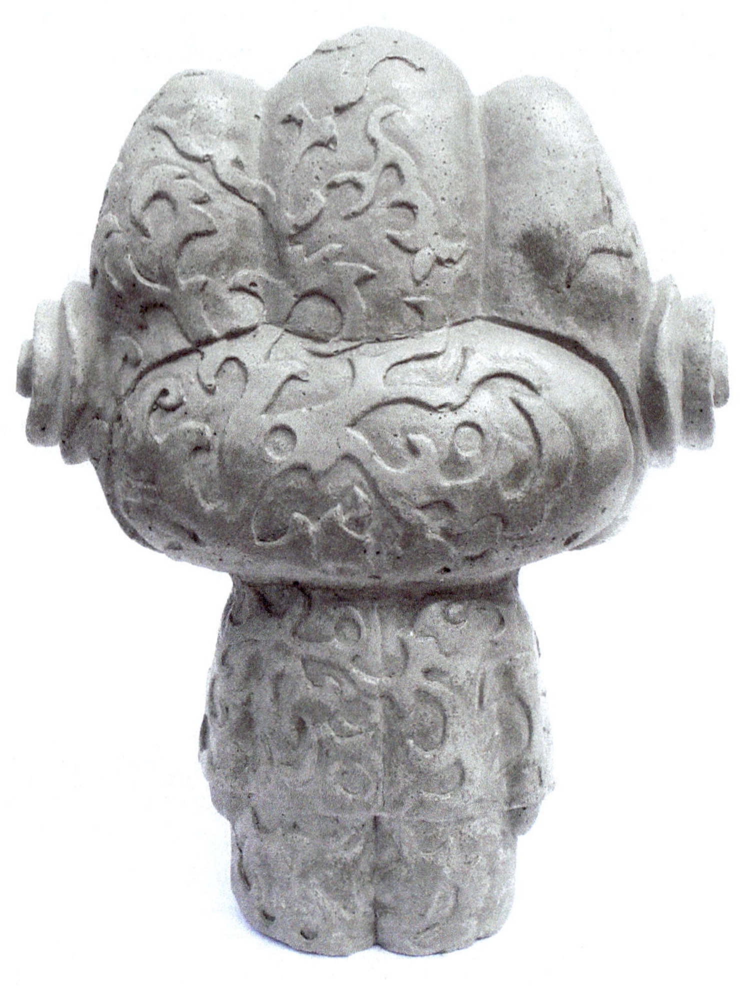

Figure 12. Rimma Arslanov, *Tank Driver*, 2007, Gray cement and sand.

the destructiveness of militarism. It also reflects the formation of the artist's own gender identity, on the seam between the girl playing with toy soldiers and the politically conscious woman who seeks to shatter fixed gender roles, as well as a clear counter stance against the deeply embedded militarism in Israeli society. With this protest against the violence represented by toy soldiers, Arslanov declares that the female voice should be included in the public discourse dominated by men with regard to issues of war and peace. Having grown up in an environment far removed from Israeli militarism in general and the country's militaristic indoctrination of its youth in particular, Arslanov's perspective offers a unique critical voice and an original artistic approach to a subject that is continuously and intensely debated both in Israeli society as a whole and among the Russian community in Israel in particular.[9]

CONCLUSION

Like migrants from other places in the world, FSU migrants face a protracted process of identity formation. This process leads to the construction of a hybrid identity in which varied and often contrary identities dwell simultaneously. This is not just an intrapersonal, subjective process matter but one shaped by dynamic negotiations with other subjects in the given society. Russian-speaking migrant women realized soon upon their arrival that they are not the sole determinants of their identity. The public's gazing eye applies a complex web of stereotypes to the newcomers, which Russian-speaking migrant women cannot escape. Whereas in the FSU it was the non-Jewish population that branded them because of their Judaism, in Israel they have become the "Russians."

Many veteran Israelis question the patriotism of Russian-speaking migrants and raise doubts about the degree of their Jewish religiosity; in addition, they ascribe to them various features that mark them as inferior. Others object to what they perceive as the sense of social superiority of many FSU migrant women, especially educated women from "White Russia." Qualities and features that have no basis in reality are attributed to their bodies, an extreme example being that of the Russian prostitute stereotype, which brands them not merely as inferior but also as immoral.

Lomsky-Feder and Rapoport's qualitative study indicates that gender is a prominent factor that influences the way in which FSU migrants form their identity and understand themselves in their new country of residence. Whereas men tend to act within the patriarchal framework of national demands and expectations (including such practices as military conscription and male circumcision), the national demands placed on women are of a more ambiguous nature (Lomsky-Feder and Rapoport, 2010: 91). They thus find independent and creative ways of self-definition that are expressed in daily life on a more personal level—in the preoccupation with their outward appearance, for example.

As I have illustrated in this chapter, art serves as an independent, personal, and creative way of dealing with the complexity of migration and the elements of the identity-construction processes of migrant women. The critical discussion of these women artists promotes a subversive exploration of what many superficially regard as Russian culture. FSU migrant women cannot be regarded as a monolithic bloc; they hail from disparate geographies and differ along many other significant axes, including class, political affiliation of right and left, and sexual orientation. There are, for instance, lesbians and queers as well as Orthodox religious women (most of whom became religious following their immigration and many of whom live in the Occupied Territories) among the FSU artists living in Israel. The women discussed in this chapter, and many others whose stories are beyond its scope, are "cosmo-refugees" in the terminology of Haim Maor, curator of the exhibition "Cosmo-Refugee: The Reflection of the Identity of FSU Migrants in Contemporary Israeli Art" (Maor, 2004).[10] In his research, Maor found that some artists choose to erase their Eastern European identity completely and replace it with an exclusively Israeli identity. Others refuse to fully adopt an Israeli identity, constructing an identity within and between the past and the present cultures. The artworks they all create thus offer a rich panorama of identities and experiences that crosses definitions of place and time and addresses life in their country of origin, their acclimatization processes, and their present experiences in Israel (Maor, 2004).

An example of the complex, multilayered, and dynamic identity of FSU women in Israel is evident in a video piece by artist Masha Rubin (b. 1973). *Vodka*, which forms part of a trilogy called *Three Short Stories*, was created in 2000 (14 minutes). The video opens with a panoramic view of a typical Russian landscape wrapped in heavy snow. A horse-drawn wagon passes by, warmly dressed children play on a carousel, and a small circus tent draws the audience in. The central segment presents a young man, standing in the kitchen of a typical old Jerusalem home;

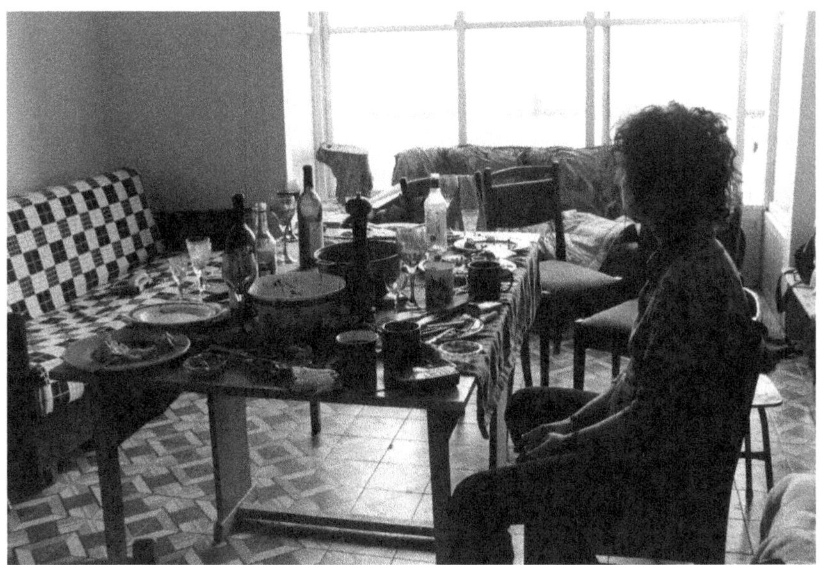

FIGURE 13. Masha Rubin, Untitled (from "3 for 10" art project), 2000. Black and white photo.

he gives a mock-serious account of the origin of vodka—the drink most closely identified in Israel with Russians—describing its long history and cultural significance. The scene is interspersed with segments from old Russian TV shows featuring folk dancing and dramatic scenes from Russian theater. Part I of the trilogy ends with scenes from a house party held for a small, tight-knit group of immigrants in Israel, one of them a lone young woman who remains after her friends have all parted (Figure 13).

In Part II of the trilogy, *Baba Yaga*, a young woman in the same Jerusalem house describes in a heavy Russian accent the features of a well-known female figure in Russian culture, the witch Baba Yaga, detailing for the viewers her dual nature—at once exceedingly wicked and kind. Interspersed are segments in which the artist's friends are shown holding a banquet with the finest Russian food—sour cream and caviar, dumplings, zwieback, and so on. In Part III, *Women*, the actress Nadia Kutcher, an FSU migrant, describes the strength of Russian women who gained positions of influence in Soviet culture. Her speech is interspersed with TV footage of communist marches and images of the revolution that feature women. The trilogy as a whole addresses gender aspects of Russian culture, offering the viewer a glimpse of this culture and of the way in which it is preserved in Israel by young women who choose to keep up Russian traditions in their new place of residence.[11] As art critic Tal Ben Zvi notes in the catalog for the "3 for 10" exhibition she curated in 2011, which featured Rubin's work:

> Rubin's film is undoubtedly diasporic art at its best. . . . It is a pseudo-documentary that serves as a "manual" for the Israeli viewer seeking to understand the "mysterious Russian soul"—an ironic "manual" that attempts to mediate the social logic of amused young migrants who speak both Hebrew and Russian. But the artist has deliberately chosen not to include subtitles when the footage switches from people speaking Hebrew to segments from old Russian films, thus leaving many in the veteran Israeli audience without the possibility of understanding the contents. (Ben Zvi, 2011)

Masha Rubin's video is but one example of the versatile spectrum of identities of FSU migrants in Israel. In Rubin's case the artist and a group of her friends have chosen to practice a Russian identity alongside their Israeli identity. Larissa Remennick's sociological studies confirm the widespread existence of such a mixed identity among FSU immigrants; some choose to continue to preserve Russian traditions by cultivating transnational ties with friends and family who remain in the country of birth, speaking Russian, engaging in typical Russian activities such as social house gatherings, attending and participating in Russian art and cultural exhibits, sending their children to extracurricular education programs run by Russian immigrant teachers, and marrying within the Russian-speaking community. Her research also reveals, however, that these trends coexist with practices considered distinctly Israeli and local, with many immigrants denying their old identity and taking great pains to assimilate fully into their new environment. These facts, Remennick believes, point to the existence of various degrees of integration of ex-Soviet immigrants into Israeli society, which in turn reflects the highly hybrid nature of their identities (Remennick, 2003). A similar position is formulated by sociologist Julia Lerner, who asserts that the great variety and differences that characterize Russian speakers in Israel are linked to their process of positioning and repositioning that creates an immense polyphony of varied voices, lifestyles, and political and ideological views (Lerner, 2012: 26–27).

The diverse artworks discussed here draw attention to situations of unease, for both the individual and the culture as a whole, revealing a powerful tension between the yearning for belonging and the desire for uniqueness and even foreignness. Each of the artists expresses a lucid voice that conveys the processes of identity formation undergone by migrant women in Israel.

The analysis of their works suggests the benefits of moving away from conceptualizing identity in terms of counter-identity formation in favor of a nonbinary picture that regards the many different groups and identities that exist in society as operating along a flexible and graded continuum. Instead of formulating the issue of migration in terms of degrees of assimilation of a migrant group into the veteran society, with the latter perceived as a static and stable group, it might be fruitful to look at all the branches of Israeli society as stratifying their identity in the face of large waves of migration and the attendant changes in the social makeup. Just as the identity of migrant women becomes hybrid when they arrive in the host country, so too the host groups are significantly influenced and changed by their arrival.

Social activist Tanya Rubinstein, a 1.5-generation immigrant from the FSU, aptly describes the prolonged process of negotiating her multilayered identity, mixing the different aspects of her identity and affiliations together:

> In my experience, every time I over-adopt one identity, I feel that it violently pushes against the other. The adoption of an Israeli identity goes hand in hand with the adoption of a stereotypical view of the migrant identity. It is associated with a demonization of the weakness expressed in the difficulty of adjusting to life in Israeli society; with the need to erase and reject my old culture. Adoption of the Russian identity, on the other hand, is associated with a defense against Israeliness; with coldness and emotional alienation; with a sense of intellectual superiority over the locals; with an ethics and way of living that doesn't pass here. . . . In the years since [my immigration], I have made this transition back and forth, each time leaning more

toward one kind of identity, then the other, and I have done this many times. Often, in the company of Ashkenazi friends, I connect with my Ashkenazi side . . . and other times, in a Russian-speaking circle, I connect with my Russian side. . . . I haven't felt complete in any of these sides. . . . Again and again, I find myself forced to choose between these two identities, my Israeli identity and my FSU migrant identity. But why do I always have to choose between them? Can't I live simultaneously with both of them? (Rubinstein, 2013)[12]

2

Israeli Women Artists

Migrants from Ethiopia

Women artists arriving from Ethiopia in 1984, 1991, and since then—who form part of the 1.5 generation—are now producing diversified artworks in the midst of coping with an ongoing threefold identity-construction process: gender, race, and class status. Many Ethiopian migrant women in contemporary Israel experience a transnational existence. They continue to maintain links with their country of origin, travel back for visits and root trips, act on behalf of others in the Ethiopian Jewish community who are also trying to emigrate and join their families in Israel, keep close contact on Internet forums with Diaspora Ethiopian community across the world, initiate commercial links, import goods and contemporary music from Ethiopia, and so on.

In this chapter I give voice to these artists through their artwork and convey the interpretations and explanations they themselves give to the pieces. The artworks constitute a rich mosaic of ideas and views as part of a canvas that encompasses the challenges and advantages of migration: feelings of difficulty and joy, failure and success, belonging and alienation. They address the ways in which women form their identities as migrants, each artist selecting and highlighting a particular aspect out of the several dimensions they hold simultaneously. Some stress the gender issues that accompany migration; others address religious aspects while drawing attention to the exclusion they experience as being Ethiopian in the Jewish Israeli collective. Some choose to create artworks that deal with the economic and class situation linked to the employment possibilities open to Ethiopian migrant women in Israel. Still others focus on the question of how Ethiopian migrants assimilate, physically and emotionally, into a primarily white society. Each work of art deals with these aspects in different shapes and forms, representing an individual subjective and critical voice.

In general, male and female artists from Ethiopia receive little exposure in Israeli museum exhibitions or art galleries. Over the years some solo and group exhibitions have been held of Israeli Ethiopian artists, such as "Jerusalem Dream from Habash," featuring a group of Ethiopian youth and women artists (Ami Steinmatz Gallery, Tel Aviv, 1989); "Assumed Identity," a solo exhibition of Esti Almo-Wexler (Beit Achoti Gallery, Tel Aviv, 2009); "Without a Name," a joint exhibition of Danny Admasso and Behrano Adams (Beit Achoti Gallery, Tel Aviv, 2009); "Covered with Banana Leaves," a solo exhibition of Tesfaye Tegegne (Man and the Living World Museum, Ramat Gan, 2010); "Revival," a solo exhibition of Benny Voodoo (Sapir College Gallery, 2010); "Stain," a solo exhibition of Or Tesema-Avraham (Artists' House, Jerusalem, 2012); and "The Journey," a group exhibition (Petah Tikva Museum, 2012). Although to date no exhibition in Israel has been devoted to Ethiopian women artists that highlights gender aspects of these women's art and lives, some exhibitions have been held in the past decade of traditional Ethiopian art, including "Gedgeda" (Hasadna Art Gallery, Rishon Lezion, 2008) and "Ethiopia: A Journey to Wonderland," which featured a variety of artistic pieces (Eretz Israel Museum, Tel Aviv, 2013).

IMMIGRATION FROM ETHIOPIA

In contrast to the relatively vast knowledge that Israeli and Western cultures have about countries from which Jews migrate to Israel (e.g., Russia, Poland, France, or Canada), many know little about the African countries in general and Ethiopia in particular. To arrive at a coherent understanding of the status and culture of women arriving from Ethiopia, we must first look at the country itself. Ethiopia has a long and distinguished history. It is one of the most ancient nations in the world, having existed as a sovereign state for thousands of years, a fact central to Ethiopian identity and heritage, as cultural researcher Jacob Gonchel explains: "Ethiopia's cultural wealth, the ancient history of a living state and government, and the fact that it is one of the oldest countries on earth—all these are a source of pride, whose trace is also to be found amongst its Jews" (Gonchel, 2005: 21).

Ethiopia is a mosaic of cultures and religions. Some seventy languages are spoken within its borders by a variety of ethnic groups. It is one of the African members of the League of Nations and one of the founding nations of the United Nations, G-77 and G-24, the Non-Aligned Movement, and the Organization of African Unity. Its capital, Addis Ababa, is the headquarters of the African Union and numerous Africa-oriented global NGOs (Teferra, 2013: 40). The country has been led for more than 2,000 years by a dynastic house as a monarchy with an organized institutional structure (Erlich, 2013: 28). Ethiopia was the third nation in the ancient world to adopt Christianity as a state religion, in 333 CE, after Byzantium and Armenia, thereby becoming one of the first places to accept monotheism. Over the generations, Ethiopia has managed to withstand the great powers of the world, including Islam and European imperialism. Along with Liberia, it is the only African nation to have preserved its sovereignty during the colonial period, the sole exception being the brief Italian rule over the country between 1936 and 1941 (29).

In 1974 Ethiopia suffered a military coup when members of the army headed by Haile Mariam Mengistu deposed the ruler, Haile Selassie, and formed a communist junta that nationalized land and municipal branches of the economy. Although the coup brought about a dramatic rise in literacy, the junta also cruelly oppressed the educated class, subjecting Ethiopia to a long-lasting dictatorship, bloodshed, and terror (Turel, 2013). Mengistu was a die-hard communist who engaged in uncompromising persecution of religion, including persecution of the Jewish community: "With the new regime clothed in a Marxist mantle, it seemed reasonable to expect the implementation of extreme measures against religion in general and separate religious groups in particular. . . . Many reports . . . during the first revolutionary years confirmed that steps were indeed being taken against certain groups—the Jews amongst them—as part of a campaign against religion" (Sabar Friedman, 1989: 247). After years of the people's struggle for national freedom, the Federal Democratic Republic of Ethiopia was born after Mengistu's deposal (Turel, 2013).

Ethiopia has long and close ties with Judaism and the Jewish people. Before Christianity arrived in the country, about half of the residents of

Aksum, in the north of the state, were Jews; Ethiopian Christians themselves believe that they are the offspring of the ancient Israelites (Turel, 2013: 20). The Beta Israel community regards itself as the descendants of the Jews who refused to convert to Christianity and preserved their original Jewish faith (Shalom, 2013: 54). They were not affected by the afflictions that visited the Jewish people after the destruction of the First Temple in Jerusalem (586 BCE) or exposed to the developments in Judaism represented by the Jerusalem and Babylonian Talmuds, the foundational Jewish texts. They have thus preserved customs and traditions from the First Temple period (54).

Whereas the Jewish identity of Beta Israel was never questioned in Ethiopia, the Jewish religious establishment in Israel was hesitant to grant the community recognition. The then Sephardic chief rabbi, Ovadia Yosef, declared them to be the descendants of the lost tribe of Dan only in 1973, a ruling that opened the gates to their migration to Israel, as diasporic Jews. When the Jews in Ethiopia obtained growing awareness of the option to go to their ancient homeland, they notified Israeli delegates of their decision and between 1954 and 1984 thousands of Ethiopian migrants arrived in the country (Adega, 2000). The two major waves, however, were Operation Moses and Operation Solomon.[1] In Operation Moses (November 18, 1984, to January 5, 1985), 8,000 Jewish migrants, mostly from the Tigray region in northern Ethiopia, arrived in Israel after trekking to the border with Sudan under terrible conditions; about 4,000 members of the community did not survive the trek (Bekya et al., 2013).

Operation Moses was halted in the middle and not completed because of an Israeli media leak that prompted the Sudanese president to withdraw his support of the operation for fear of reaction from the Arab world. As a result, 15,000 Jews were left stranded in camps in Sudan and Ethiopia, where they lived for years for the chance to emigrate to Israel. During those years, more Jews, from all over the country, were arriving in Addis Ababa in the hope of going to Israel. In early 1991 a chance for change in the stagnant situation occurred, because the rebel forces in the country were getting closer to Addis Ababa and Mengistu's communist regime was facing a crisis (Erlich, 2013: 35). The Israeli government, fearing that Mengistu's imminent deposal would spell disaster for the thousands of Jews waiting to be brought to Israel, opened negotiations with Ethiopia to get the Jews out of the country as quickly as possible.

Eventually, an agreement was reached in May of that year allowing them to leave. Therefore a new operation started, titled Operation Solomon, which began on May 24, 1991, and lasted 34 hours. During that time, the Israeli Air Force and El Al planes transported 14,300 people to Israel (Turel, 2013).

Operation Solomon and the fall of the communist junta in Ethiopia occurred at the same time, and the migration of the Ethiopian Jewish community was part of a broad process of change in the Ethiopian regime. This in itself formed a link in the collapse of communism worldwide that signaled the beginning of the transnational era and mass waves of migration across the globe.

The Ethiopian Jews who came to Israel now number 138,200 (Central Bureau of Statistics, 2014)—a small community compared with the approximately 1 million FSU migrants who came during the same period. They nonetheless gained high visibility in Israeli society, which views them with a large measure of ambivalence.

EMPLOYMENT

Over the past decade an ever-growing number of Ethiopian Israelis have succeeded in entering a range of professions in the civil service and the free market sector. Their level of academic education, which facilitates social mobility, has significantly increased, in particular among the younger generation. Jobs regarded as prestigious in Israeli society are clearly integrating a growing number of Ethiopian Israelis. Despite this positive trend, however, members of the Ethiopian community encounter employment problems that demand attention and resolution.

Artist Sofia Jambar (b. 1981) considers the issue of employment among Ethiopian migrants in general and migrant women in particular. She has created a series of photos documenting security guards in a large commercial operation. Figure 14 portrays a female security guard employed by a contracting firm. She is photographed standing in the room where the guards get ready for work and leave their possessions during their shift. The photo articulates a reality that is simultaneously gray and colorful, representing the grave occupational world of many Ethiopian migrants in Israel. The backdrop—a strangely colored, surrealistic-looking room whose walls are painted pink, yellow, and blue—reveals the behind-

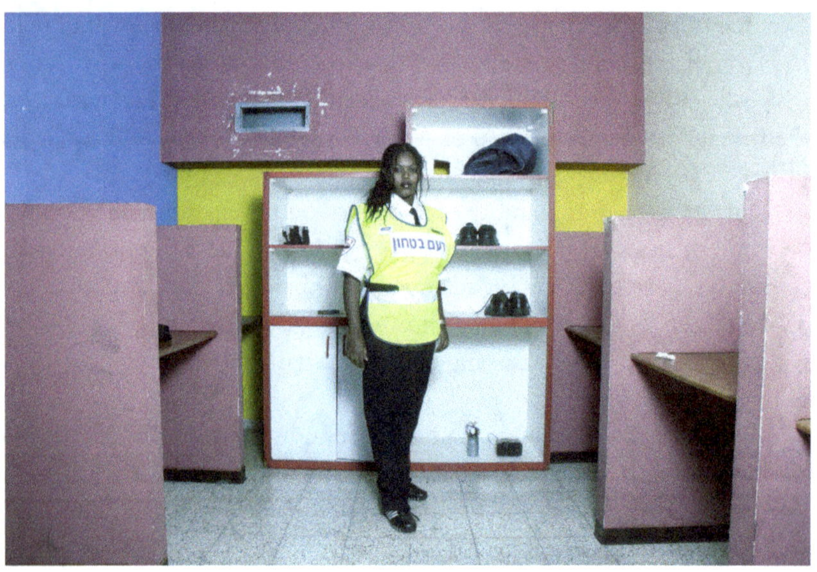

FIGURE 14. Sofia Jambar, Untitled, 2006. Color photo.

the-scenes refuge of the gray, overlooked, transparent people who check bags for weapons and ensure public safety in shops, restaurants, malls, and banks.[2]

Jambar describes the marginality these women suffer in such jobs: guards employed by contracting firms under exploitative terms and no employment security. The artist insists on documenting her subjects in the service room in which they get ready for their shift, where they are hidden from view, rather than at the main entrance to the shopping mall, where they perform their actual job. This back service room space physically and metaphorically depicts their invisibility and transparency, evoking the fact that they exist in the backyard of the employment world in Israel.

As researcher Orly Benjamin (2011) notes, workers in nonprofessional fields, both in the free market and in the civil service, are vulnerable to exploitation. Contracting firms exploit the system of tenders and trend toward privatization to control an increasing share of the nonprofessional market sector in a way that undermines women's working conditions, particularly those of migrant women, and adversely affects the work market as a whole. A survey conducted by economists Erez Sinibar and Gil Epstein in 2012 (cited in Weisberg, 2012) indicates that Ethiopian migrants with no professional experience receive the lowest wages in Israel, a status previously occupied by Israeli Arabs. This circumstance derives, the two contend, from the fact that Ethiopian migrants face cultural gaps and limited work opportunities. In contrast to FSU migrants or the Arab sector, where additional employment possibilities exist in the community itself, "Ethiopians have less possibilities and labour leverage via intra-community contacts" (Weisberg, 2012). Although these employment difficulties face both genders alike, the values held by the community and society at large make immigrant women, particular elderly women, more at risk of unemployment or extreme exploitation. Many of the migrant women seeking work outside the home find menial, low-paying jobs, working as security guards, office cleaners, cashiers, and supermarket packers.

The Mahut Center, an organization that seeks to improve the economic status of women in Israel, published a report, *Women Workers in a Precarious Employment Market*, that highlights the gender aspect of low-paying labor. According to the report's authors, "Women who earn low wages face special difficulties that affect their lives and well-being as a whole. . . . Beyond their severe economic distress, they feel insulted and trapped. The first sense derives from the absence of any link between their work investment and pay cheques, the second from their knowledge that they will rarely—if ever—find good working conditions and sufficient income" (Buchsbaum et al., 2008: 59). Many women who have entered the workforce as low-paid workers resign themselves to being exploited, frequently not even expecting to gain in the future a fair recompense for their labor (61).

Until recently, the policy of the Israeli establishment was not to encourage migrant Ethiopian women to integrate into the employment market, especially women older than 45. As sociologist Esther Herzog notes in her study *Immigrants and Bureaucrats: Ethiopians in an Israeli Absorption Center* (1998), absorption officials regard the Ethiopian community as a conservative and traditionalist social group marked by a clear and firm hierarchy within the family: the father and grandfather standing at its head and the women underneath the male figures. Position papers written over the years in relation to absorption policy have thus determined that migrant Ethiopian women turning to employment outside the home would cause the collapse of the family structure and child neglect. These position papers assert that men should not be expected to carry an equal share of household duties when the women work outside the home. The argument has also been made that, because Ethiopian women do not earn a proper wage, it is better to strengthen them in their home and intracommunity context rather than try to improve their working conditions (E. Herzog, 1998).

In Ethiopia the status of women in society is mixed, split between a conservative process that constricts them to the home and empowerment activity that draws them into the public sphere. In general over the course of history, women have been responsible for traditional gender roles, such as child rearing and housekeeping. They have also been responsible for heavy physical tasks. The clear difference in social status between men and women in Ethiopia is exemplified by the lack of opportunities women have to acquire an education or develop economic independence.[3] These disparities are anchored in the country's civil law, for example, the right to own land and the laws of inheritance (Abate, 1991).

Numerous studies of the issues of gender inequality point in particular to education as a direct source of the lower status of women in Ethiopia. Over the centuries and even up to today, most Ethiopian women live in rural areas and do not receive the same number of years of education as their male counterparts. According to a 1976 Ethiopian governmental survey, even women living in the big cities and employed outside the home generally suffer from gender inequality, earning a much lower wage than men in the same jobs, including those known as being low paid (Abate, 1991).

In recent decades a change of awareness has begun to take place in Ethiopia with respect to the inferior status of women, and the government has begun efforts to correct the situation. Thus, for example, an official government document issued in 1998 stresses the need to empower women in order to encourage social progress in the country as a whole: "Ethiopian women are actively involved in all aspects of their society's life. Women are both producers and procreators and they are also active participants in the social, political, and cultural activities of their communities. Economic development is unthinkable without the participation of women" (Women's Affairs Office, 1998). However, the varied and important roles Ethiopian women play have not always been recognized. The discriminatory political, economic, and social rules and regulations prevailing in Ethiopia have barred women from enjoying the fruits of their labor. Without equal opportunities, they have lagged behind men in all fields of self-advancement.

A survey conducted in 2008 summarizing the status of women in Ethiopia over the past decades reveals a complex and stratified picture. The surveyors examined the different spheres that various types of women inhabit—Christians vs. other religious groups, urban vs. rural, and so on—and analyzed static indexes, such as level of education, level of exposure to the media, level of knowledge regarding contraception methods and protection against disease, views relating to the age of marriage, and employment and wages. All the indexes indicated that significant gender inequality still exists in Ethiopia today, affecting all sorts of women (UN Population Fund, 2008: 16–33). This study proves that, although the situation of women is improving, much work still remains to be done before equality is achieved. This complex view sharpens the need to investigate the differences between various groups of women in Ethiopian society and to find solutions and varied tools to meet their diverse needs.

With respect to the status of Jewish Ethiopian women, Israeli sociologist Esther Herzog adduces a more complex and multidimensional explanation than that of the state. She argues that the division of labor in the Jewish family in Ethiopia was not rigid but fluid and flexible; the domestic and public spheres were not always rigorously maintained. Thus, for example, Herzog reminds us that in Ethiopia sewing and weaving were traditionally male occupations. Upon the migrants' arrival in Israel, however, these skills became a female preserve, and the system directed all the women into specified courses in which they learned the housekeeping skills that wives and mothers are customarily expected to master in the Western world. Israeli policy thus forced them into Western stereotypical gender roles (E. Herzog, 1998).

Contra Herzog, Leah Kacen and Malka Shabtay maintain that the status of Jewish women in Ethiopia closely corresponds to their non-Jewish counterparts. According to them, Jewish women lived in patriarchal societies in Ethiopia, constituting a minority in large cities and the majority in small rural communities. "The division of labour with the family was clear: the man was the authority figure and he represented the family within the community and to its leadership. As the most respected person in the family, he was responsible for its economic situation, the distribution of tasks, education, and tradition. The woman—who married at a very young age—moved to live with her husband's family and was regarded as his property. Her work involved very hard manual labour and she was responsible for cooking and raising the children" (Kacen and Shabtay, 2005: 62). When the community migrated to Israel, the need to adapt to Western forms of life led to great changes in their traditional lifestyle. The men lost much of their status in the new country; their wives were the first to seek work outside the home. The women thus adjusted to their new circumstances more quickly than the men, mastering the Hebrew language, dealing with the authorities, and running their daily lives.[4] Many young Israeli Ethiopian women also enlist in the army or do national service, focusing their efforts on gaining higher education and attaining key positions in organizations and agencies, various academic professions, and the employment market in general (64).

EDUCATION

Despite the patronizing and oppressive policy of the state toward older immigrant women from Ethiopia, who were encouraged to stay at home and not enter the Israeli workforce, a more active line has been adopted with respect to the new generations in the hope that they will integrate into Israeli society as quickly as possible. But this hope was itself nonetheless accompanied by patronization and oppression, for upon their arrival in Israel, many teenage children were sent to boarding schools, away from their families, in the belief that their parents would hold them back and that they would be better off in institutions (Yakir, 2005: 34). This phenomenon forms part of the state policy (Glasner, 2005) that regards Ethiopian migrants as a high-visibility group and a unique bureaucratic category, one that is frequently represented as a "special-needs group" (Antebi-Yemini, 2010: 55). Ethiopian immigrants are often the subject of arrogant and racist treatment and have been described as a "social problem" in the national press (Wertzberg, 2003). Health workers constantly warn that they (re)present serious health hazards, and clerks in the education system classify them as requiring special help (Tuval, 2004). Young Ethiopian immigrants' encounters with the Israeli education system can hardly be described as successful; many studies and publications draw attention to the huge, mostly negative, influence that the education system and establishment in Israel have on their self-image (Demle, 2011; Salamon, 1997; Swirski and Swirski, 2002).

In 1991 all Ethiopian immigrant children were automatically enrolled in the religious education system in their catchment area, with all those older than 12 attending boarding schools run by the Youth Aliyah Department (Antebi-Yemini, 2010: 56). This no-exemption policy exemplifies a lack of trust in the parents' and community's socialization skills. As Shula Mulla, an educator and social activist in the Ethiopian community who personally experienced the policy, notes, "Today, I understand that the [Jewish] Agency sent us, the children, to boarding schools because they thought that in this way they would 'save' the children from their 'primitive' parents and families" (quoted in Yakir, 2005: 34).[5]

A series of works from 2008 by artist Dana Yosef (b. 1979) includes portraits of some of the young girls whom she accompanied as part of her job as an Ulpana coordinator in the Binyamin District. In her painting *Angudai*, she portrays a girl with short-cropped hair sitting rapt in her own thoughts, contemplating and pondering a point that disappears into space (Figure 15). "In this series of paintings," Yosef observes, "I wanted to raise a complex and

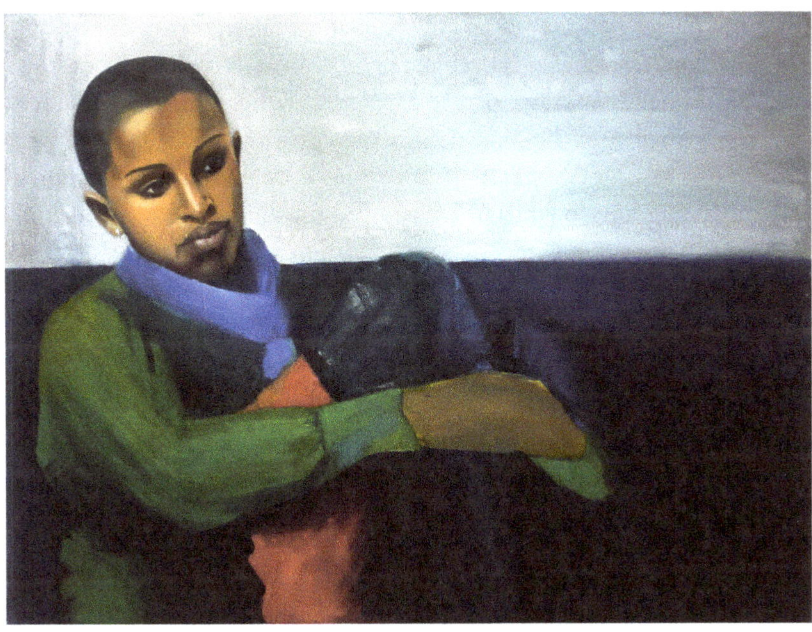

FIGURE 15. Dana Yosef, *Angudai*, 2008. Oil on canvas.

painful issue—the state of Ethiopian youth within the Israeli education system" (Yosef, personal correspondence, 2012). The series of paintings depicts the young girls she educated over the course of two years who became a significant part of her life. The students, she elaborates, have to cope with integrating into a foreign country, adopting to a new culture, and going through the conversion process, all while being disconnected from their families—in essence, being required to form a new identity while experiencing a broad range of complex emotions, including loneliness.

The assimilation and education process in the boarding school, which is far from the students' homes and families, adds to their conflicts of identity, increases the intergenerational gap, and undermines the traditional Ethiopian family structure. Sending Ethiopian youth to boarding schools is part of a strategy that the government regards as helping this population to integrate. As Esther Herzog remarks, however, it in fact forms an inescapable trap: "The idea of 'help' holds an important place in constructing the patronage and dependence created by the state authorities between themselves and the categories considered as being in need—Mizrahis, new immigrants, single parents, the disabled, disadvantaged, etc." (E. Herzog, 2007: 133).

Yosef relates that the young girls who appear in the series of paintings are not the direct or central theme, because, as far as she is concerned, they do not represent tragic personal cases but rather attest to deliberately tendentious policies. The image of the girls serves as a way of raising the subject of the integration and assimilation of the younger generation of Ethiopian migrants in Israel by focusing on the difficulties and challenges they face in the various stages in the education system.

> I wanted to draw attention to the cost a migrant girl has to pay and the things she has to sacrifice. Frequently, she has to give up her independence and become passive in order to be accepted in her new culture. I feel this is true of both genders, all members of the community, but the women in particular are forced to choose and sacrifice in order to integrate. In the case of young women, the price is especially high and very heavy. In addition to all the choices and sacrifices they have to make, they face a reality in which they have to be less than what they are in order to survive. (Dana Yosef, personal correspondence, 2012)

In the catalog of the exhibition in which Yosef's works were shown, the curator, Orit Adar-Bechar, writes, "In her paintings, Yosef looks at girls from a realistic-lyrical viewpoint that derives from her long acquaintance with them and the empathy she feels for their situation. While she paints glowing compositions that exhibit the influence of the American artist Edward Hopper, at the same time the present, influenced by the Israeli circumstances, is very evident in the very personal, close-up view of their distress. The girls are depicted as though they are detached from reality, closed, and cut off from their new environment" (Adar-Bechar, 2009). Affirming this interpretation, the artist commented, "The concepts that come to me from the paintings are alienation, segregation, frozenness, and passivity—alongside growth, activity, hope, and diligence. So in this way, together, they hold a past, a present, and a future" (Yosef, personal correspondence, 2012).

SKIN COLOR AND BLACKNESS

Some current studies in social science, such as the one conducted by Nissim Mizrachi and Hanna Herzog, indicate that typically Israelis of Ethiopian origin avoid mentioning their blackness in an attempt to enter into larger Israeli society (Mizrachi and Herzog, 2012: 427). Nonetheless, most people in Israel point to black skin color to identify Ethiopian Jews, leading to their characterization as Others (Antebi-Yemini, 2010; Shabtay, 2001). Skin color became one of the dominant ways in which the Ethiopian community was defined—by the migrants themselves and by veteran Israelis.[6] The extreme emphasis on black skin color by veteran Israelis is an unambiguous and gross display of biological racism (Shenhav and Yonah, 2008) based on biological physical features. This form of racism assumes a link between attributes such as skin color or body and facial structure and mental qualities, such as intelligence, motivation, and ethics.

It is nonetheless important to remember that skin color is a relative rather than a firm and essential category. Interestingly, the blackness of the Ethiopian migrants was born, crystallized, and formulated only with their arrival in Israel (Dahan-Kalev and Maor, 2015). Thus, for example, sociologist Antebi-Yemini, maintains that, in their own color scheme, Ethiopians regard themselves as reddish brown rather than black, only undergoing a change in visibility after their migration, when the "blackness" attributed to them became a prominent feature: "The immigrants went from being non-striking Jews in Ethiopia to identification as black Ethiopians in Israel" (Antebi-Yemini, 2010: 45–52).

Because the black identity of Ethiopian Jews is present in the works of many Ethiopian migrant artists, it is worthwhile reviewing the historical and cultural use to which the concept of blackness has been put. Its historical origin lies in the social movement known as Négritude, which arose in Paris in the 1930s. Négritude was formed by black artists, writers, and poets living in French society as an opposition movement to white racism. Its members highlighted the African's uniqueness, emotions, and closeness to nature and the earth. Many other black people of the time, however, had great reservations about the character and essence of this black outlook (Shenhav and Yonah, 2008: 31). Thus, for example, Frantz Fanon, a Martinique-born French psychiatrist, philosopher, revolutionary, and writer who was one of the formulators of postcolonialism, described the catch-22 of being trapped between the essentialist view of blackness as elaborated by the movement's leaders on the one hand and the color black as a "metaphysics" in which the black person is entrapped on the other (31). Today, the politics of identity offers ways of dealing with this trap, such as "color blindness," which suggests that we remove all reference to skin color in language, or the efforts to create a multiracial and multicultural society.

One of the most prominent principles of postcolonial discourse is strategic essentialism, a temporary tactic used by a group to accentuate its unified identity in order to advance its political interests and represent itself to others. Although its members may be diverse and belong to several subgroups, the "essentialization" of the group qua group for political purposes—for a short, delimited period of time—enables their cooperation and collaboration. In this context, unity is perceived as constituting an effective tool for achieving one's goals. Strategic essentialism makes it possible "to hold both ends of the rope: to reject the ontological status of the black man and create a counter-political entity" (Shenhav and Yonah, 2008: 33).

Today, "blackness" serves not only as a physical description of skin color but also as a definition of a conscious political and cultural state. Africanism joins blackness as a geographic, historical, and cultural referent, all these together forming a vigorous and fruitful critical discourse across the globe. In the context of the lives of Ethiopian migrants in

Israel, blackness is treated in a dual fashion: the reason for their exclusion and the discrimination they suffer and an indicator of their uniqueness, tradition, and pride. Some people use the term *black* to express political anger; others use the term as a mark of respect for their African roots and traditions—in such a way, however, as to weave the context into their present environment and lives.

This complex attitude and relation to blackness is also reflected in works of art. Most of the artists under discussion give a prominent place to the various aspects of blackness enfolded in their lives, challenging the hegemonic Israeli view and overt expressions of racism by means of reclaiming images of black femininity. These images conduct a critical discourse with the stereotypes that label the figure of the Ethiopian woman as Other in Israeli society and the collective desire to whiten and thus merge them in the Zionist melting pot project. These artworks function as a form of self-examination in which the black woman, traditionally regarded as the object of the hegemonic gaze, investigates her own image, reclaiming the gaze as she interprets and represents herself through her own viewpoint.

The works of Esti Almo-Wexler (b. 1980) challenge prevailing Israeli hegemonic images. In a piece created in 2006, she constructs an imaginary image of a black woman who looks straight toward the camera while her naked body is covered with large, broad green leaves (Figure 16). Using leaves to cover the naked female body has traditionally been a generic symbol of Eve, the first primitive, sinful woman. Only the simple, industrial youth bed—a conventional, prevalent bourgeois piece of children's furniture—against which the figure reclines situates her within the framework of contemporary Israeli reality.[7] The playful position of the image, a sort of biblical Eve in the Garden of Eden, reveals the parody and performative aspects of the staged photograph, enabling the viewer to understand, process, and reconstruct the way in which the image was created. This tactic removes color from its essentialist status, presenting it as a cultural construct (Butler, 1990). The neutralization of the "natural" characteristics of color mocks the cultural stances the viewer ostensibly holds and, in effect, the issue of ethnicity itself, pulling the carpet out from under the notion that the body is the exclusive source of recognition (Spivak, 1998). In other words, the presentation of color as an unreliable, or at least dubious, witness anticipates a new and independent identity category, of which color is not the primary signifier.

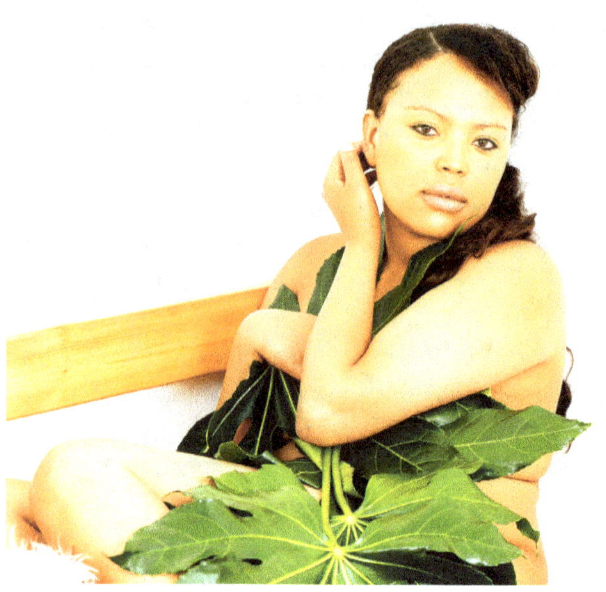

Figure 16. Esti Almo-Wexler, Untitled, 2006. Color photo.

The photo exhibits affinities with the prevalent white Israeli narrative regarding the Ethiopian community, a narrative that holds that black culture is primitive, indecipherable, and shrouded in mystery. This attitude recalls the patriarchal-chauvinistic stereotypical stance regarding the woman as a mysterious creature, as opposed to the logical, rational male. Like the ideas propounded by African American theoreticians and activists such as Angela Davis, Audre Lorde, bell hooks, and Patricia Hill Collins, Almo-Wexler removes the divide adduced between racism and sexism and highlights the double oppression to which black women are exposed. In contrast to feminists who refrain from linking racism and sexism and lay claim to universalist femininity, feminists of color expose the diverse structures of oppression that intersect in the life of the black women living in a white patriarchal society.

In another work, from 2006, Almo-Wexler presents black skin as the antithesis of whiteness (Figure 17). In this photo a black woman is wrapped in a long white robe; an opaque white curtain falls behind her, and a bowl of plastic fruit is placed on a pseudo-classical pedestal by her

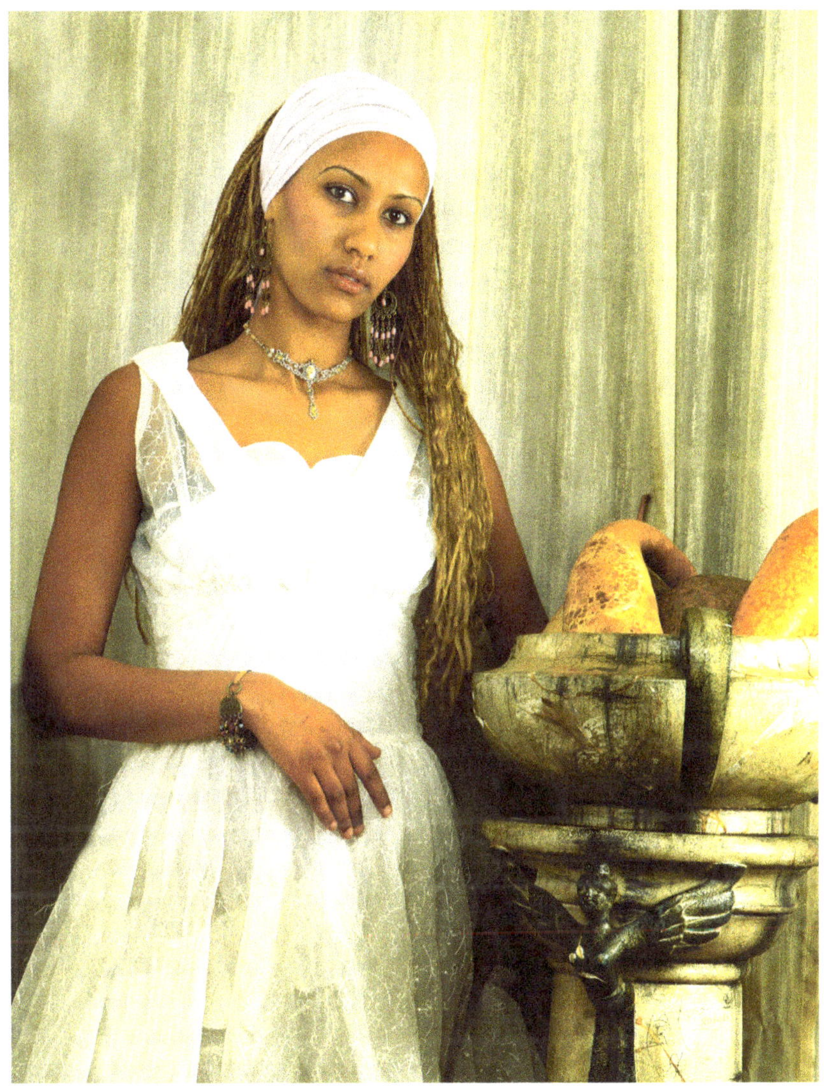

FIGURE 16. Esti Almo-Wexler, Untitled, 2006. Color photo.

side. The tension of the contrasting effects created by the binary colors of the image—black vs. white, gold, and yellow—diminishes the black skin to a dark stain in the composition.

This artistic choice draws attention to the idea of whiteness as a transparent, self-evident, all-embracing, universal space in Israeli society

(Shenhav and Yonah, 2008). Within this framework the color black is regarded as a dominantly negative force that glosses over individual differences and other distinctive signs that set one person off from another. Black creates an inclusive, stereotypical, automatic identity, such as the objectifying calls "Dirty nigger!" or simply, "Look, a nigro!" described by Frantz Fanon (1967: 109) and other black writers and theoreticians.

The photo in Figure 17 suggests that, against the surrounding whiteness, black skin turns the figure from a real woman into a labeled, stereotyped image. The message is clear and simple: Blackness becomes a monolithic category set in contrast to the color white, functioning as a sort of meta-color upon which the body is clothed. The choice to present a feminine figure, as in most of Almo-Wexler's images, accentuates the sense of absolute otherness, representing the intersection of identity categories: national, ethnoracial, and gender oppression.

Artist Smadar Elias (b. 1981) also presents resistance to the stereotypes from which Ethiopian people, and Ethiopian women in particular, suffer in Israeli society. Elias voices this opposition through a form of artistic language that makes symbolic use of prevalent notions of black and white, their physical inversion transforming their meaning. In a photo made in 2006, she presents a deliberately distorted self-portrait of a female image outside the focus of the camera lens (Figure 18). The upper part of the figure's body is wrapped in a towel, her hair is bound tightly behind her, and her black face is painted white, producing a simultaneously delicate and grotesque appearance. The artificial whiteness highlights the playful intersection between her black face and the white mask, which Elias links to the idea of the Western ideal of beauty: "This is me photographed with a 'beauty mask' on my face, a white mask on my black skin" (Elias, interview by author, 2008).

This correlation reveals the pain inflicted on countless people facing the rigid standards of beauty and the impossibility of achieving it under the conditions stipulated by Western aesthetics, in which whiteness constitutes the default of beauty. In this context the figure's towel accentuates the "exposed body"—the body as it is, stripped of all the cultural attributes that symbolize its cultural belonging. It also hints at the act of washing, which may itself be read as an intimate symbolic act of purification, although full "purification" from blackness can never be achieved. As Fanon notes, the mask serves as a metaphor for the act of the integration

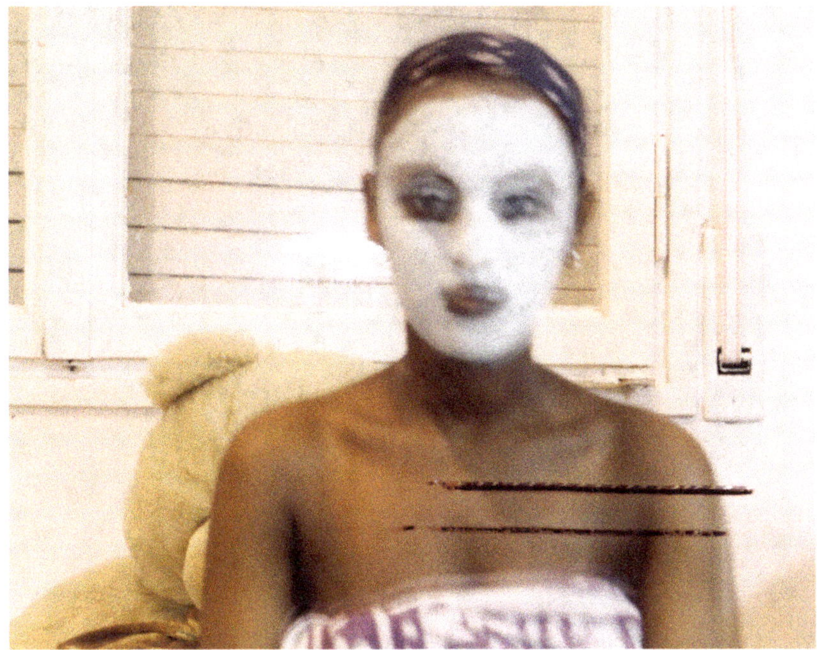

FIGURE 18. Smadar Elias, Untitled, 2006. Color photo.

of blackness within hegemonic white culture because "the white man is sealed in his whiteness. The black man in his blackness" (Fanon, 1967: 9).

In another work Elias portrays her own head as bursting out of the top of a massive tree (Figure 19). This piece, charged with irony, presents a woman with a freestyle Afro hairdo against a rainbow shining in the background and an ancient-looking tree deeply rooted in the landscape of an imaginary African savanna. The photo reconstructs the stereotypical representations of blackness—primariness, primitiveness, genericness—that correspond to "nature." Although Elias turns her gaze toward Africa, the contents of the piece are political rather than nostalgic. The link with Africa echoes contemporary African postcolonial discourse that strives for auto-emancipation and an independent culture not discussed or thought of in relation to any other.

African postcolonial thought developed among thinkers, poets, and writers within and outside the African continent, primarily during the second half of the twentieth century. In contrast to the Western perspec-

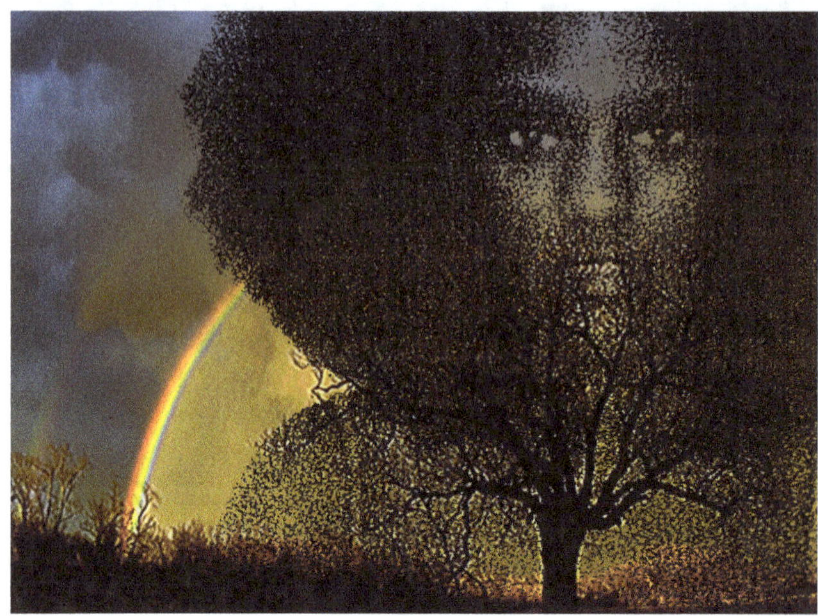

FIGURE 19. Smadar Elias, Untitled, 2007. Manipulated color photo.

tive, which divides the world into regions and conceptualizes this division in terms of below and above, oppressed and rulers, first world vs. third world, developed vs. developing world, the African discourse offers a complexity of intersections, making use of insights drawn from the anticolonial struggle that took place on the continent. The thinkers and activists who propound this approach seek to rename situations of conflict, trauma, internal wars, eradication, and even migration that occurred in Africa rather than think of them in terms of or in relation to events and processes occurring in other parts of the world. As cultural researchers Dalia Markovitch and Ktsia Alon remark, the African postcolonial discourse seeks to undermine the concept of hybridity that is expressed in terms of an exotic subject, an exciting mixture of carnivalesque elements. According to the African discourse and critique, the "hybrid subject" reveals the inequality of the claim that local culture, considered inferior, can or should join forces with "superior" white, Western culture. Unlike the postmodern trends that have eroded that discourse in the West, the African discourse thus refuses to adopt the "celebration of hybridization" as a cornerstone (Markovitch and Alon, 2005: 5).

Reappropriation of an African denied identity and the dismantling of a hybrid identity not only have been the monopoly of the inhabitants of the African continent but also have been promoted over the past two decades in other places and communities across the globe, including Israel. Such attempts at identity formation are particularly significant in light of developments in various fields, for example, academia. The framing and definition of the white gaze on the black is given graphic expression in the Israeli academic discourse: Despite its small size, the Ethiopian community has been the subject of intense scholarly attention, primarily in the field of anthropology. The studies that have gained highest visibility, greatest academic esteem, and largest budgets have, in the main, been conducted by white scholars writing about Ethiopian immigrants and their descendants. The hegemonic discourse consistently assumes the normative experience in Israel as the de facto universal, neutral, modern point of reference. This yardstick is applied to Ethiopian migrants, using indexes said to be "objective," such as housing, employment, education, military service, and health (Brookdale Institute, 2001; Shabtay, 2006). Some studies of Ethiopian migrants a priori frame Israeli Ethiopians as an inferior community. By doing so, they reveal their own lack of self-critical awareness; the authors do not acknowledge themselves as "Frangi" people (i.e., foreign white people) who do not belong to the "target" group and fail to position themselves in the context of the unequal and often discriminatory power relations. Although these studies claim to represent and act according to ostensibly universal indexes, they are biased and therefore problematic. The extensive scholarly literature regarding the Ethiopian population in Israel thus frequently constitutes an anomaly and distortion.[8]

The situation in Israeli academia sharpens the importance of independent moves toward identity formation, with many encouraging signs of this trend being visible on the ground. Alongside the plethora of hegemonic studies of Ethiopian migrants there exists a significant trend that does not fall within the focus of white scholars or the white public at large. Many of the 1.5 generation are now coming of age, gaining college education, and formulating their feelings and stances by and for themselves. Extensive research, books, Internet sites, and cultural contents are thus now being written and created from the Ethiopian community's own perspective. These sources are primarily designed to serve a platform for the Ethiopian community's members and to serve as a tool directed toward the veteran Israeli community. Among these I note the My Ethiopia and YES blogs, the Israeli Ethiopian television channel (IETV), the dance troupe Beta, and the Israeli Ethiopian theater Hologeb.

When Smadar Elias places an imaginary Africa as her central image, she seeks to reject the Eurocentric gaze that local white hegemony imposes on blacks, turning them into the Other. She makes a clear distinction between blackness and whiteness, striving to formulate black culture as an independent entity.

In another work Elias reverses black and white by reworking an old family photo. Taken soon after the family migrated to Israel twenty-five years earlier, the photograph shows her father and mother and four of their children, all standing formally erect and frozen in front of the camera. A digital process that the artist uses turns the positive image into a negative; the final result produces an effect of a surprising whitening of the images (Figure 20). Elias regards this reversal as a symbolic act embodying the racist social reality of Israel: "I took the original photo and turned it into a negative—and then everything becomes a play of black and white, like the reality here in the country" (Elias, interview by author, 2008). This reality was sharpened by the critical feedback to the work. Elias received many surprised responses prompted by the photo's manipulation: "I remember that when the photo was exhibited, someone came up to me and asked why I had photographed Swedes—white people" (Elias, interview). This question embodies a patronizing stance that assumes that Ethiopians should confine themselves to depicting things they understand, that is, black-skinned people. In this photo Elias draws attention to the playful dimension of color, reminding us that color is a shifting, nonstable notion that at the same time has concrete and deep meanings and effects that are stamped on the body and the soul.

Although critical, Elias's photograph can be ascribed to a broad sociopolitical trend that seeks not only to understand and present color and gender as oppressive in nature but also as possessing positive and empowering sides. This trend identifies blackness and femininity as unique signifiers and the source of the recognition and strength of the gender and ethnic position that black women hold (Dekel, 2013: 75–79). In Israel, Mizrahi feminist discourse (Lir, 2007) and Palestinian feminist discourse (Ghanem, 2008) are two of the most prominent representatives of this

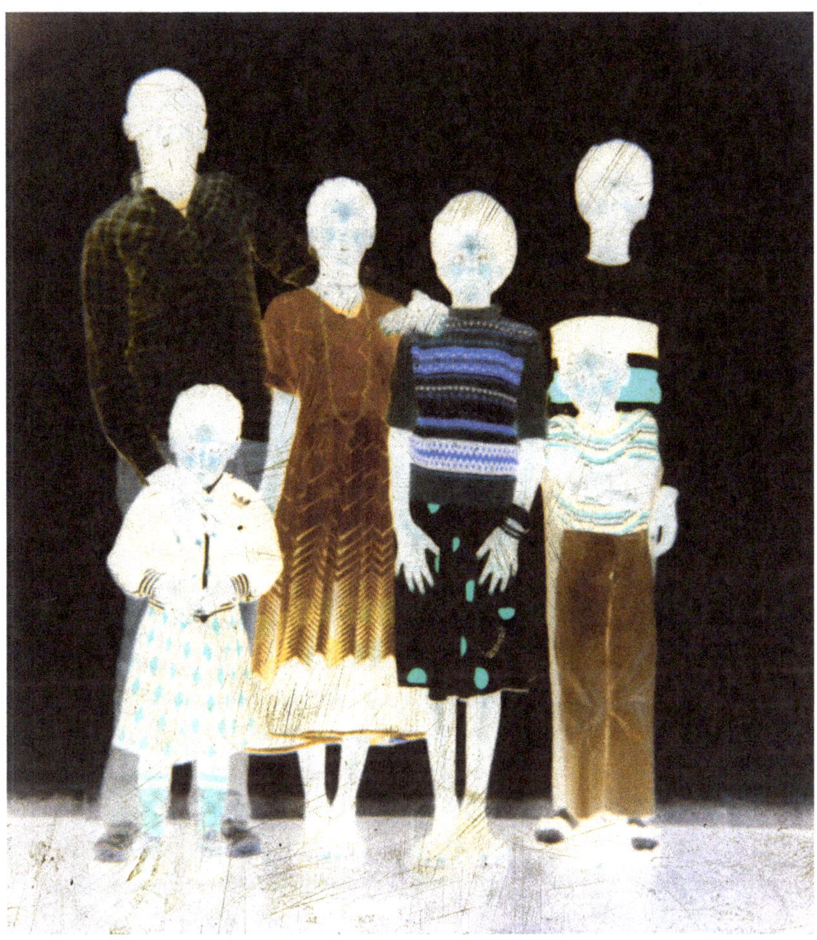

Figure 20. Smadar Elias, Untitled, 2007. Manipulated color photo.

position, drawing their inspiration from the theory, politics, and activism that have developed across the world since the 1960s (Rogoff, 2000).

The theories and activism of black feminism in the United States gave birth to many artistic works, such as those of the African American artist Faith Ringgold (Raven and Ringgold, 2004). Such works also influenced the growth of contemporary African art on the African continent (Fall, 2007). Undergoing a paradigm shift, this has led to the grounding of the unique voices of contemporary black women across the globe. In Israel the work of Mizrahi women—also inspired by these global developments—found expression for the first time in 2000, in two exhibitions curated by Shula Keshet. The first, "Achoti: Mizrahi Artists in Israel," was held at the Artists' House in Jerusalem; the second, "Mizrahiyot," was held at the Ami Steinitz Gallery for Contemporary Art in Tel Aviv. As Ktsia Alon observes, this was "the first, groundbreaking time when the feminine Mizrahi artistic voice—as a distinct, unique voice—became publicly visible" (Alon, 2013: 115). These pioneering exhibitions gave visual expression to gendered Mizrahi identities both as a political stance and as a self-representation of blackness.

For Smadar Elias, too, the transforming act of "whitening" the members of her family in the old photo represents her complex process of identity conceptualization.

> It's not simple . . . to present it like this, your family, because they're dark-skinned. If you present them in this way, whitened, it's as though, perhaps, you're mocking them, or something like that. . . . I look at this piece from a conscious, critical place. I'm now grown up, an adult, and yet things haven't changed here—the absorption of the Ethiopian community hasn't occurred as it should have, and this is my way of expression and of presenting the issue. It's not simple to stretch your family out on a huge picture of a meter by a meter and a half in this way. But this gives a much stronger effect. The question is, What will remain of this issue in the end? (Elias, interview by author, 2008)

GENDER AND RACE, ART AND CRAFTS

In many places around the world, negative representations of black people are reinforced by oppressive gender notions and negative representations of women. These two categories are also prevalent in Israel, flowing over into diverse cultural fields, including the arts. Throughout history, creative women have been pushed into the domestic realm of activity (Beauvoir, 2010) and thus have been excluded from the cultural creativity of the public sphere (Nochlin, 1988). From the perspective of patriarchy, the artistic activity that women perform falls primarily into the category of traditional craft, which is of merely decorative use. Embroidery, sewing, pottery, and weaving belong to the prominent traditional enterprises ascribed to this field (Parker and Pollock, 1981). Most of the artworks discussed in this volume, in contrast, make use of artistic tools that are considered Western: photography, video, performance, installation, and painting. Several Ethiopian women artists have expressed a critical attitude toward this artificial dichotomy.[9]

In 2010 artist Tigist Yosef-Ron (b. 1976) produced a series of pieces, originating in photographs she shot, in which the central image is a young girl. She titled these *Noa* after her oldest daughter (Figure 21). Yosef-Ron digitally processes the image and prints it on canvas; then she embroiders the figure's contour lines and dress with red thread. Speaking of these works, she comments, "I really like craft work. I like working with my hands. These are things my mother used to do. But I incorporate it in a different, contemporary, way. I take it to my own places, which describe my own circumstances, taking care to stay away from old, 'used' places" (Yosef-Ron, interview by author, 2010). Yosef-Ron intends to enlarge the works into broad canvases, such as those used on public billboards: "At the moment, they're small pieces, but I'm planning big ones—huge white canvases onto which I'll stitch red threads. They'll be like stretched nets onto which enlarged images can be projected. These works rely heavily on graphics—by profession, I'm a graphic designer. They are in fact the precursors to huge embroidered works—but in a very graphic, hi-tech style" (Yosef-Ron, interview).

Yosef-Ron seeks to combine two gendered dimensions in her art—the mother-daughter relation and the degradation of feminine work. The mother-daughter bond is a unique, delicately woven relationship carefully constructed from fine, yet strong, threads. Like finely embroidered pieces, the task of motherhood is painstaking and arduous, demanding energy, attention, and time. Yosef-Ron also uses her art to protest against the devaluing of women's work in patriarchal society. Rather than using the traditional form of embroidery, her works represent a critical and reflective act: "I started the project with the memory of folklore and my mother's traditional craftwork. Although it's linked to an abundance of colors, it evolved into something else as I chose to work through the prism and contemporary language of computerized graphic design. In this way, the traditional style was refined and condensed. It's a filter of years in the business of graphic design that led things to become minimalistic, almost monochromatic. All the magic of childhood and the maternal link are

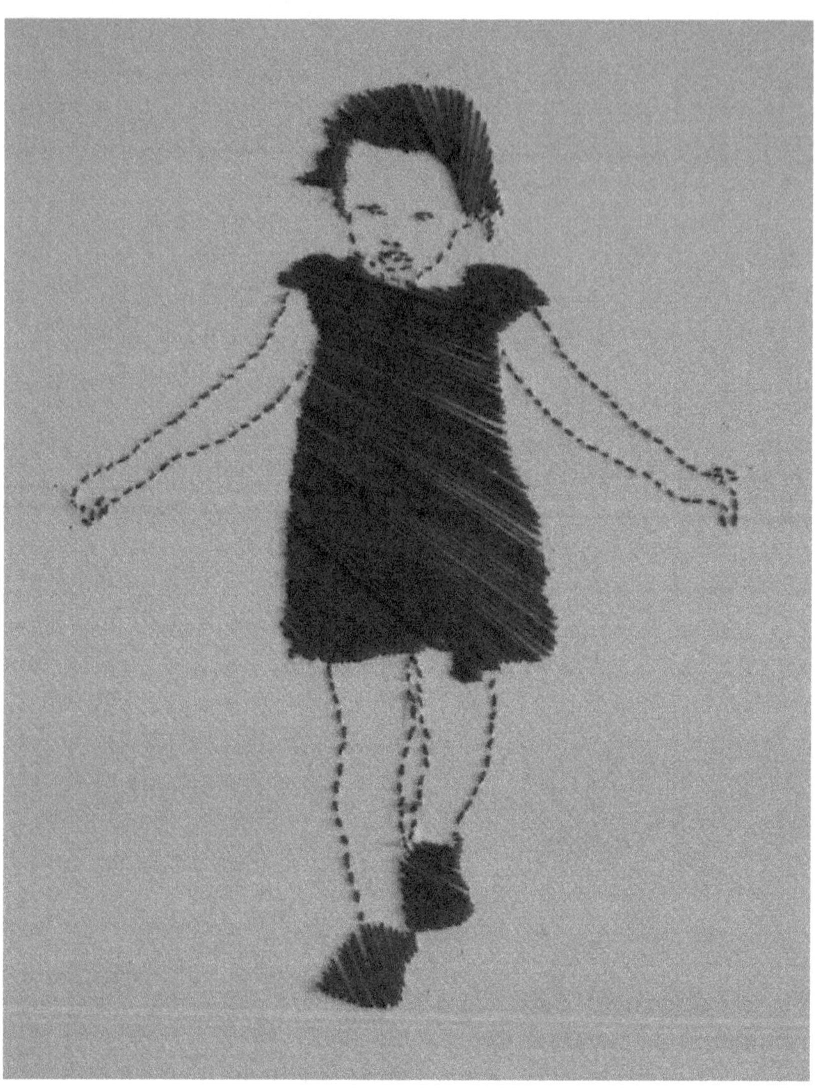

Figure 21. Tigist Yosef-Ron, *Noa*, 2010. Mixed media.

expressed in modernistic language, with very few succinct lines" (Yosef-Ron, interview by author, 2010).

In her recent works, Yosef-Ron has focused on subjects related to gender in general and motherhood in particular, painting her daughters, female friends, and images of mothers with their babies.

BLOOD AND RACE

Blood has formed a significant cultural and religious symbol throughout history, as evinced in endless wars and acts of vengeance, blood alliances, and such slogans as "Blood is thicker than water." Together with issues of race, blood becomes even more charged. Artist Elsa Gedamo-Tegegne (b. 1982) created two video pieces that relate to the theme of blood and race. In one (untitled, 2008, 5:01 minutes), a black woman is kneeling on a standard white kitchen floor while the camera focuses on her palms and well-manicured, red fingernails (Figure 22). The hands make a repeated rubbing motion against one another as they are dipped in a red liquid, as though she is washing them. In the background the sound of the viscous liquid trickling can be heard, like a strange, disturbing effect. According to Gedamo-Tegegne, this represents the endless and purposeless attempt to clean the body from stains and dirt (Gedamo-Tegegne, interview by author, 2010). The camera's focus on the black hands and their glittering red-polished fingernails engaged in cleaning

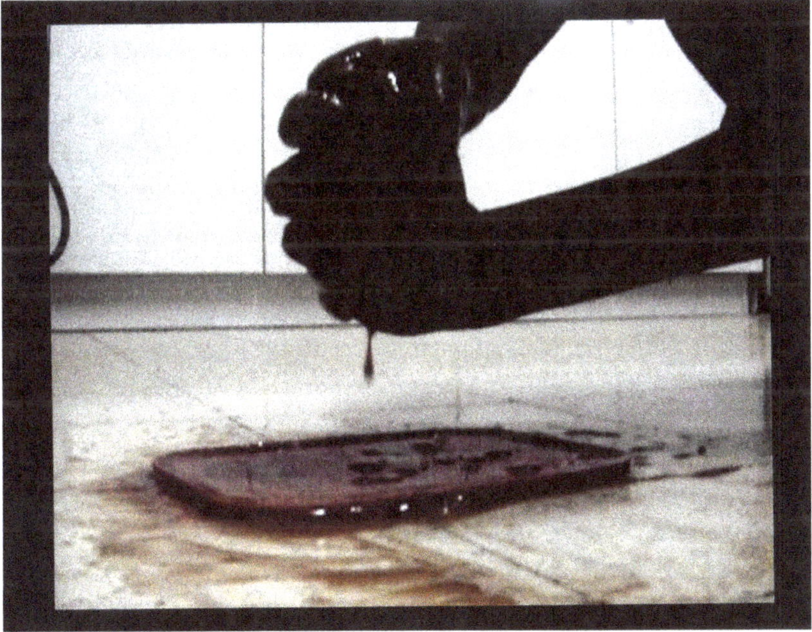

FIGURE 22. Elsa Gedamo-Tegegne, Untitled, 2008. Detail from a video.

the kitchen sharpens the female gender characterization. The polish is a symbol of feminine cultivation; the kitchen is a symbol of the space traditionally assigned to women. The link between the manicured hands and the cleaning maintenance that dirties them and breaks the nails symbolizes the inherent contradiction that marks women's lives. On the one hand, cultural constructs compel them to be manicured and groomed; on the other, they are condemned to perform all the normative gender roles assigned to housewives and cleaners.

The piece highlights not only domestic spaces and their maintenance but also feminine self-engagement with the body. By choosing red liquid, Gedamo-Tegegne evidently refers to the subject of female menstruation and social attitudes toward this physical phenomenon; thus the video addresses the social-patriarchal stances toward femininity.[10] According to Jewish law, menstrual blood and the menstrual period possess a special status. In Ethiopia the women of Beta Israel were accustomed to separating themselves in a menstrual hut during their menstrual cycles and after childbirth (Cicurel and Sharaby, 2007; Yanai and Rappoport, 2001). These were situated in a prominent place in the village; their centrality enabled the members of the community to oversee the women's fertility. When the Jewish community moved to Israel, the menstrual hut disappeared as the community's patterns of habitation altered. In the beginning the women did not know how to practice this custom. Over time, however, those who chose to continue it found places in the home to replace the hut, such as a separate room for the woman during her period and after childbirth (Antebi-Yemini, 2005). Within the community it is thus evident that great importance is attached to blood and the menstrual cycle as formative elements of feminine identity.

Another of Gedamo-Tegegne's video works also deals with the subject of blood (untitled, 2008, 3.25 minutes). In this piece the camera lens focuses on red drops dripping onto a white wall. Although the image is readily self-evident, the filmed scene does not easily yield to decipherment—viewers are left with a feeling of confusion and disorientation. After some minutes, they begin to decode the visual symbol that is constructed by means of a dual reversal: the drops are dripping upward, against the law of gravity, because the frame is inverted and turned upside down. The film itself is also played backward, the drops thus flowing outward from the wall toward their place of origin. At the end, then, the wall appears completely clean. In the background is the sound of a well-known Ethiopian lullaby, sung by the artist herself. As Gedamo-Tegegne explains, this song is taught to young children in school, and her singing of it here symbolically accompanies the transition from the innocence of childhood to the harsh outside reality (Gedamo-Tegegne, interview by author, 2010).

Gedamo-Tegegne's comments regarding "sobering up to reality" could be related to the broader sociopolitical context of the deep trauma that Ethiopian migrants experienced in what is known as the blood libel affair. Between their arrivals in 1948 and 1996, when the affair was first exposed by the national daily paper *Ma'ariv*, all blood donated by Ethiopian migrants for the national blood bank was systematically destroyed in line with a directive issued by Magen David Adom (the Israeli Red Cross); this directive was concealed from the Ethiopian donors altogether. Media exposure of the affair aroused an indignant public response and the creation of a public national committee of inquiry. The policy of use or nonuse of blood donated by people living in certain countries—or who had lived in these for a certain amount of time—is, of course, an accepted practice in many blood banks across the world. Thus, for example, for a long time Israelis who had lived in Britain were not allowed to donate blood for fear of having been infected with foot and mouth disease; other potential donors from African countries were also refused because of the prevalence of HIV/AIDS on the continent.[11] In the case of Ethiopian migrants the injustice lay primarily in the concealment of the fact that they were not accepted as donors, especially in light of the fact that blood donation constitutes an act of human solidarity bound up with a sense of national identity and services to fellow Jews in need. They perceived the secretive rejection of their blood as an attempt to exclude them from feeling like full and equal citizens, "real" Israelis. Together with the broader significance that blood has carried with respect to Jewish identity, religion, and culture over the centuries, the community—while still living in Ethiopia—regarded blood as a significant symbol that distinguished them from their Christian neighbors through the rules of kashrut and slaughtering practices; because eating blood is forbidden, the blood must be drained. Their sense of religious and national exclusion was therefore extremely deep (Ben-Eliezer, 2008).

Gedamo-Tegegne's video represents harsh criticism of this act of exclusion, metaphorically depicting difficult feelings through a process that seeks to describe the effort to clean the unwanted blood smeared on the white wall that has colored everything red. The artist symbolically describes the infeasibility of washing away the signs of blood or achieving the degree of whiteness required for acceptance in Israeli society (Gedamo-Tegegne, interview by author, 2010).

In the catalog for the graduates' exhibition in which Gedamo-Tegegne's pieces were shown, the artist chose to include several personal comments about them. Under the heading "Immigrant in the Corner," she explains:

> I come from a culture in which we are accustomed to hiding rather than showing our emotions. Revealing one's feelings is considered a loss of self-control. The social mandate regarding the public demonstration of emotions is expressed in the well-known saying: "Hod holon Yichele—the stomach carries everything." . . . The pieces I created are meant to encourage people to express the feelings induced by the socialization process we experience as immigrants. But the process of revealing emotions encounters resistance from both veteran Israeli society and the Ethiopian Jewish community itself. It thus begins each time anew from the starting point. (*Catalog of Graduates of B.A. in Art*, University of Haifa, 2008)

In these two video works, Gedamo-Tegegne reveals loaded feelings, thereby breaking the social taboo customary in the Ethiopian community. At the same time, she also undermines the prevalent stereotype of Ethiopians as nice, quiet, and restrained people held by white Israeli society; the works openly express the difficult emotions Ethiopian migrants feel toward the recipient society and at the same time criticize the gender discrimination and exclusion from which women suffer.

FROM GIRLHOOD TO WOMANHOOD

In her graduate exhibition of 2010, Or Tesema-Avraham (b. 1983) exhibited a series of photos, letters, and video works dealing with the question of migration and cultural integration through the experiences of Ethiopian Jewry, the women in particular. Its central part consists of three self-portrait photographs of the artist with a traditional white embroidered Ethiopian dress (Figure 23). As art critic Smadar Sheffi notes, "The artist stands naked, holding—not wearing—a dress, as a

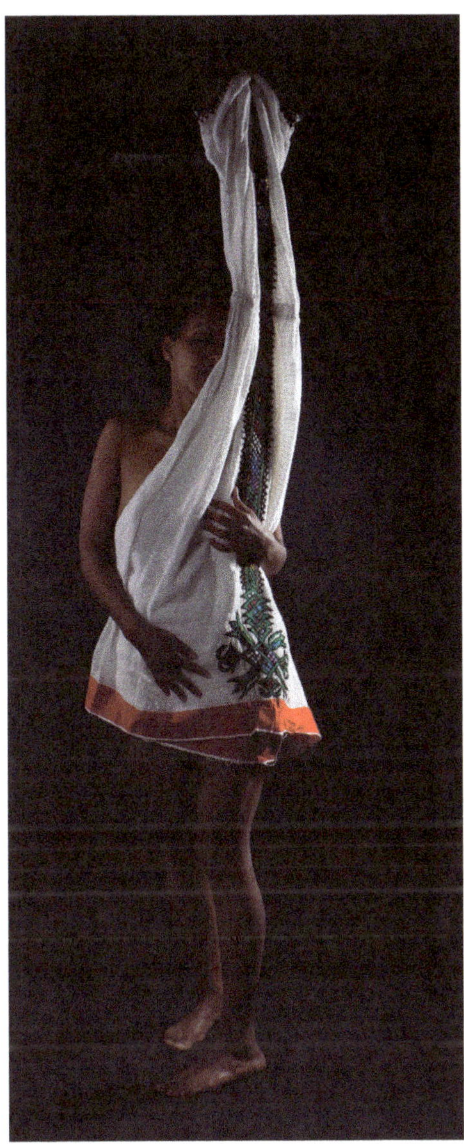

Figure 23. Or Tesema-Avraham, Untitled (one of a series of three images), 2010. Color photo.

concretization of the ambivalence and duality between alienation and proximity to her tradition" (Sheffi, 2010: 17). The artist's choice to present a dress and a naked female body is testimony to her strong interest in the gendered perspective of the community's immigration.

In a 2012 exhibition titled "Stain," Tesema-Avraham chose to present only young female images, through which she invited viewers to

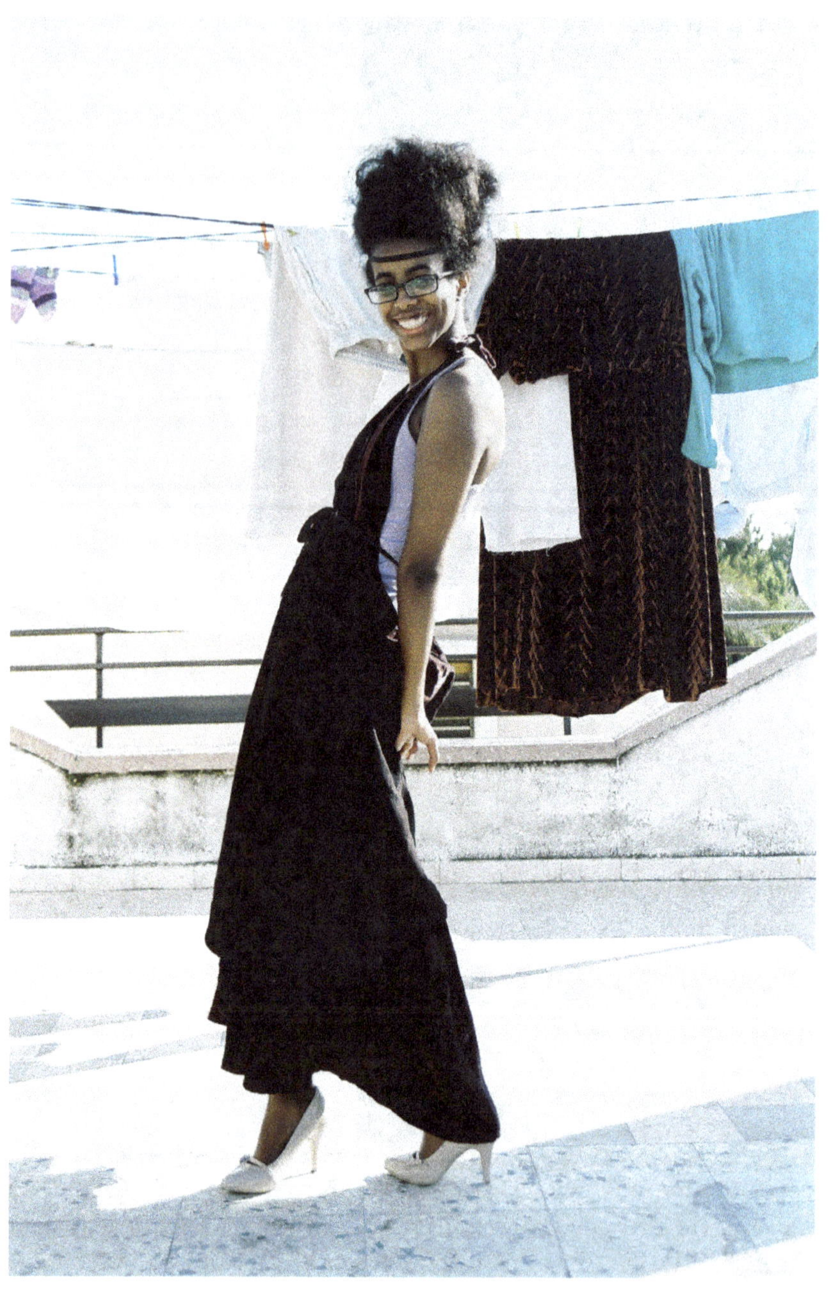

Figure 24. Or Tesema-Avraham, Untitled, 2012. Color photo.

reflexively contemplate puberty as experienced by young immigrants, serving her as a sort of autobiographical perspective. In one of the photos a young girl wears a long, oversized dress and high-heeled shoes that are too big for her feet (Figure 24). Sheffi suggests that the girl's twisted torso, turning backward, recalls the poses of professional models in the advertising industry that are regarded as sexy and that the girl wishes to imitate those poses (Sheffi, 2012: 17). The photo is one of a series of portraits of the artist's nieces—13- and 14-year-olds—in which the girls wear oversized, "grown-up" items that they themselves chose for the purposes of the filming (Tesema-Avraham, gallery talk, 2012). The artist explains that, although the girls had chosen the outfits they believed express femininity, their clumsy immaturity is clearly manifested through their gestures: "I did this series of photos because I was really interested in this transitory stage into womanhood" (gallery talk, 2012). The exhibition's curator, Eyal Perry, argues that the photographic perspective serves as an analogy for the artist's own girlhood, puberty being the starting point of a personal journey into womanhood and adult life, which occurred at the same time she embarked on the migratory journey to Israel. It thus represents a critical, reflexive examination of the period she experienced as a young teenager in the new country she had come to, at a time when she was simultaneously forming her female and national identity—a dual challenge far from a simple identity-construction process (Perry, gallery talk, 2012).

The pivotal piece in Tesema-Avraham's graduation exhibition of 2010 was a self-portrait (Figure 25). In this photo the artist sits on a wooden chair against a dark background that contains no other objects. Her eyes gaze directly at the camera; her hands lie close to her side, and her knees are whitened by what might be abrasion or the residue of white coloring. As Tesema-Avraham commented in a gallery talk in honor of the exhibition, the image originated in a childhood memory in which she saw a pupil punished by his teacher, who forced him to squat on his knees on painful gravel. Watching the injustice, she went to help the boy, helping him sit up. Many years after the incident, which persisted as a traumatic and formative memory, she reconstructed this theme with her own body, justifying the choice of the subject thus: "People expect a woman to be on her knees and I decided that I don't agree with this. I decide to stand upright" (Tesema-Avraham, gallery talk, 2012).

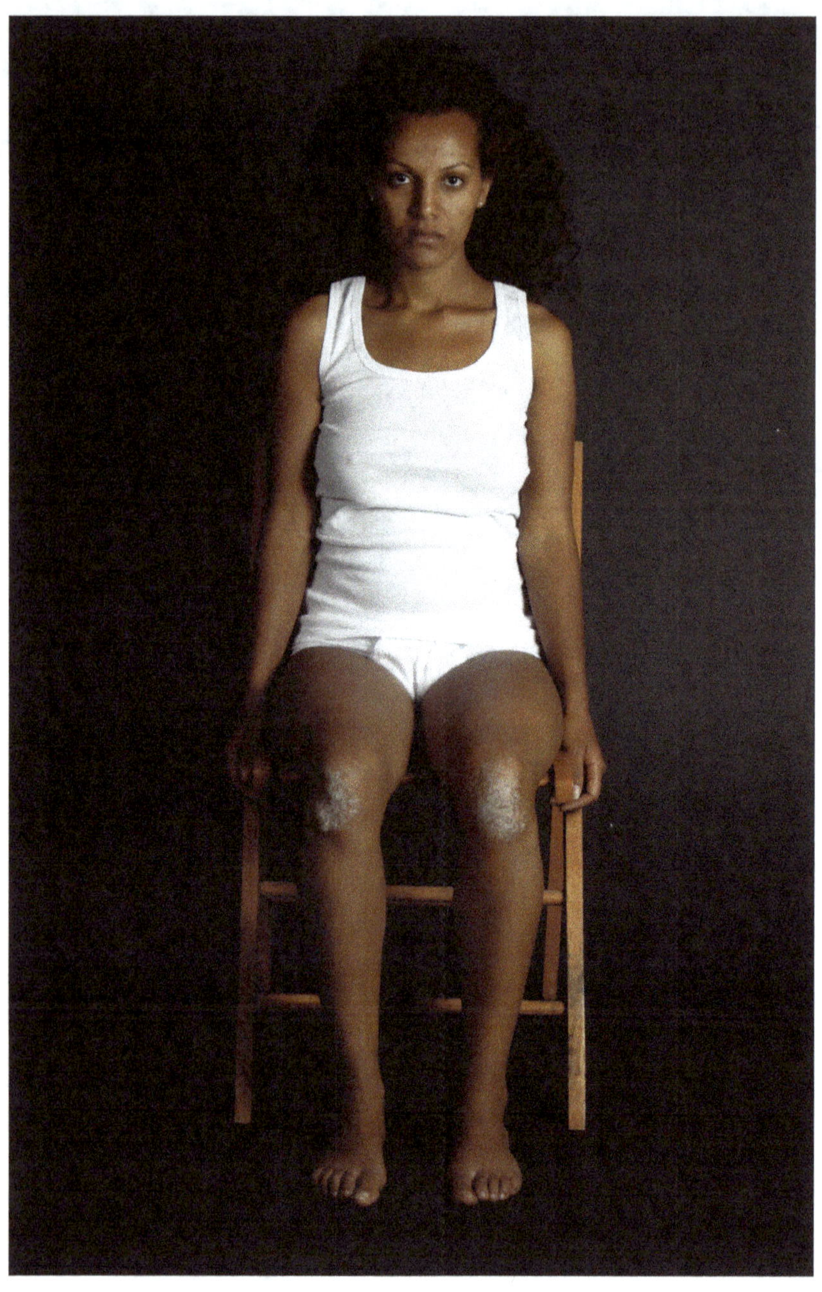

Figure 25. Or Tesema-Avraham, Untitled, 2010. Color photo.

The decision to wear an undershirt and underpants designed for men on her female body allowed the artist to represent a fluid and vague gender identity, freed of restraints and the cultural constructs customary of the binary-categorical notions of femininity and masculinity. These pieces of clothing might also echo the Israeli visual image of the socialist kibbutz pioneers, the young boys and girls walking around in unisex underpants and undershirts. This is possibly a critical view of the ostensibly egalitarian and asexual utopian ideas that the kibbutz and Zionist ethos sought to inculcate. These in fact have not been able to withstand the test of reality in modern Israel, which is now rife with sexist and misogynistic attitudes. By wearing such typical underwear, she reclaims the white, male Zionist kibbutz ethos for her personal narrative, thereby making her presence felt as a hybrid subject. Appropriating the images reserved for kibbutz boys and girls of Western origin, she expropriates the exclusivity of the white European Zionist narrative, as though declaring, "I'm also a part of the Zionist fabric."

CONCLUSION

Although they are often regarded as a monolithic group, the artists discussed in this chapter cannot be organized under a unifying category because such a grouping exists only in the cultural imagination. In reality, the young artists hold a variety of worldviews and beliefs and have divergent experiences. After graduating from art academies, some of them chose not to continue their studies but to create their artworks independently, remaining creative and fruitful artists; others decided to continue on to gain master's degrees. Their choice of themes and perspectives—such as religious faith, motherhood, relationships and membership in a community, or employment, careers, and incomes—all differ. For this reason, we cannot include all of them in a single, homogeneous entity or draw conclusions and make generalized assumptions regarding the nature of the "group" or the ways of thinking and acting we might expect of its members (Minh-ha, 1989).

Some of the artists focus on the recipient society's attitude toward Ethiopian migrants; their work addresses ethnoracist issues through a gendered lens. Others choose to highlight the subjects of economy, employment, and various gendered issues of class. Some elect to examine the feelings that arise from women's interpersonal relationships in the community, endeavoring in particular to depict and characterize female family ties, such as the mother-daughter bond. Still others prefer to concentrate on puberty issues and the transition to womanhood. Interpreting this transition as a formative social element, they illustrate in their works how this gender dimension is affected by ethnic and racist aspects. Each of the artists makes heard her own clear, individual voice, which expresses an active agency, and their creations serve as a tool of reflexive and critical elucidation of the subjects that are of interest to them.

As in every migrant group, the artists evince complex relations with the recipient hegemonic society. On the one hand, they desire to be integrated and assimilate into it; on the other, they wish to retain their distinctiveness by preserving their roots and traditions. Each artist finds her niche along this continuum. Identity definition is always an ongoing process, one that is directly affected by multiple positionings and variables (such as historical, gendered, or class parameters). Within this context a multilayered identity is formed that derives from the tension between exclusionary and inclusionary forces.

Sofia Jambar, for example, created a series of photographs that focus on the preparation and ritual practices of drinking Ethiopian coffee and another large series of photographic images relating to the Sigd festival celebrated every year in Israel.[12] One photo from the Sigd series, which documents a communal happening in honor of that festival, reflects a multilayered reality that expresses various power relations (Figure 26). At the bottom, on the ground, is the figure of a woman. Above, on a speakers' platform, is a male figure. The woman is dressed in traditional clothes, the man (the politician Adiso Masale) is clothed in a Western suit. The woman's eyes are closed, her gaze directed deep inside herself; the man looks to the horizons, over the crowd listening to him. The antithetical gender images represent a series of opposites in every possible sense—physical positioning, attitude toward attire and tradition, action and agency, and even the question of the gaze. All these create a resonating dichotomy that covers the range of identities and positionings in which the Ethiopian community exists in Israel. An additional level, that of the wider community of Israeli citizens as a whole, is represented by the national flag in the background, which contextualizes the situation in the Jewish state—the backdrop and cause alike for the enlargement of the range of

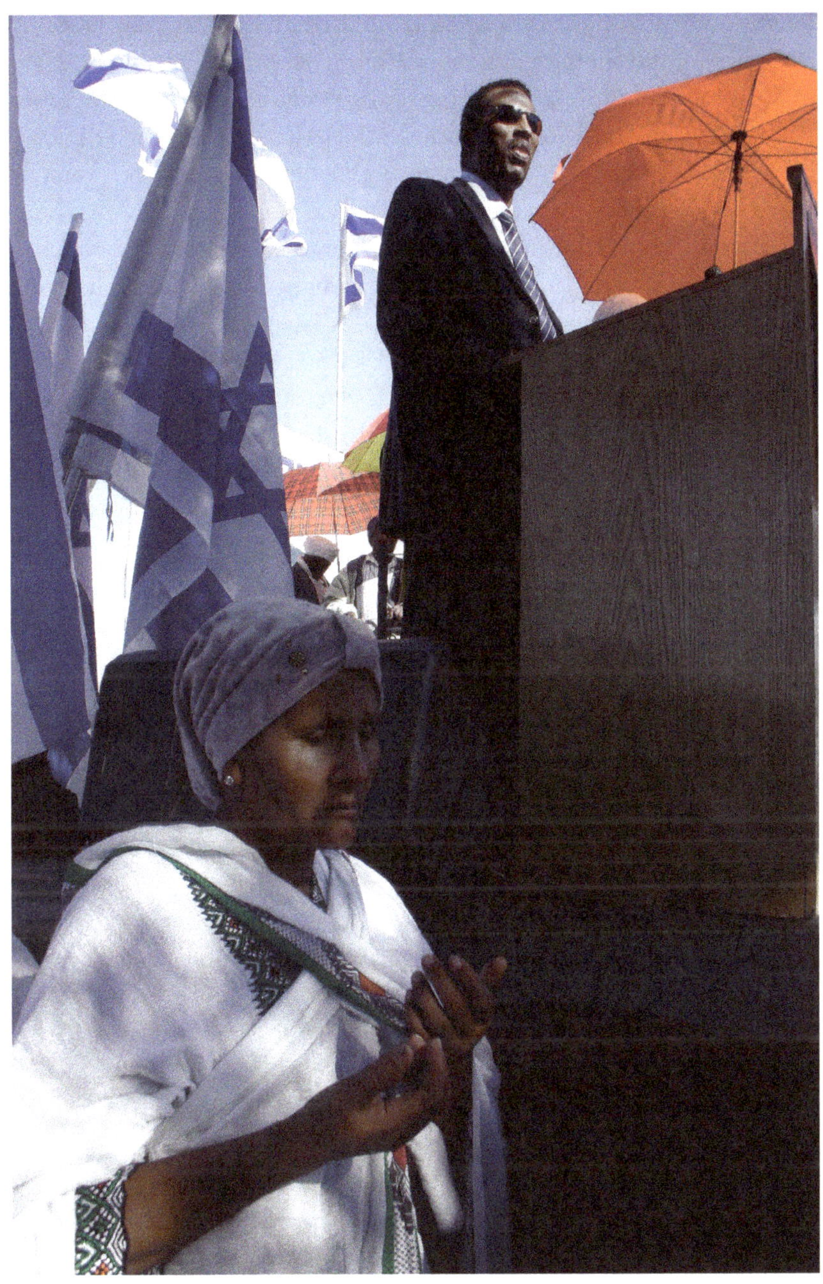

Figure 26. Sofia Jambar, Untitled, 2007. Color photo.

identities. Jambar presents a critical, sophisticated gender view based on awareness of the complex politics of identity that shifts between belonging to Israeli culture and belonging to one's original culture and between being a man and being a woman in this society.

Jambar's voice is only one of many in the field. The identity formation processes of young women, members of the 1.5 generation who came from Ethiopia in their girlhood, line up in an independent, nonoppositional row, presenting an alternative subjectivity that shakes itself free of the hegemonic framing. This position is consistent with the suggestion of the African American thinker bell hooks, who claims that the alternative community can be built only from those who do not hold a binary world view of "we" and "them" (hooks, 1990). In similar fashion, Pnina Raday, one of the participants on Alon Misganaw Demle's Facebook page, later turned into a book, elucidates the ambivalent feelings of identity that the Ethiopian community in Israel experiences—also her own—which might be described as hybrid.[13] Under the heading "Only we will define who we are," Raday states:

> The whole subject of the acceptance of the Other in Israel is extremely problematic. I, too, feel completely Israeli. Sometimes there are people who try to undermine my sense of this. I don't let them, however. . . . What's sad is that in every group you'll find a subgroup whose members don't feel as though they belong. For example, amongst the religious, there's no connection between the Religious-Zionists and the Ultra-Orthodox—or between Sephardi and Ashkenazi Ultra-Orthodox or the Ultra-Orthodox and Reform or Conservative Jews. The same happens amongst immigrant groups. . . . But I do know one thing: It's not worth waiting for veteran Israeli society to accept the Other. That'll only happen in another twenty years, if at all. I say: make a decision that you belong to this space that's called "Israeli society" and behave as though you've been here since the founding of the State. It's a shame to wait until someone gives us the feeling that we belong. . . . No one has exclusive rights over the term "Israeli" and I don't know how far we'll succeed in educating our environment. But in the meantime we'll take responsibility by feeling that we belong. (Demle, 2011: 74–75)

3

Filipina Artists

Migrant Workers in Israel

The artwork of female migrant workers opens a window onto the lives of women who, coming to Israel to find work, live on the seam between two worlds: the temporary country in which they live now and their original homeland. The experiences of Filipina women in Israel are particularly valuable for understanding the complex obstacles many migrant women confront, because Israel is an ethnonational state that strictly excludes the possibility of non-Jewish citizenship or assimilation. This group of women, marginalized from the public sphere and their lives and experiences hidden from the public eye, are brought to center stage in this chapter, their art giving expression to their lives.

As is common in the increasingly transnational world, in which migrants relocate worldwide while preserving relationships from afar, Filipina migrant workers in Israel maintain close social and economic ties with their homeland. They cultivate continuous links with family and friends by means of the Internet, keep up with political events back home, take part in Filipino events organized by the local migrant community, celebrate national Filipino holidays, and buy Filipino foods and goods. At the same time they celebrate Israeli national holidays, enjoy local foods and culture, and make friends with veteran Israelis.

In Israel, female migrant workers are defined as foreign workers. Officialdom divides them into two groups. The first group, the subject of the present discussion, includes those who were encouraged to come. They arrived to fill specific jobs, and they possess official work permits and are employed by manpower agencies. They are thus legal workers, invited by the state on a quota system, and most aspects of their lives are regulated by the Israeli legislature. This group also consists of women who had a working visa but lost it for some reason and those who entered the country on a tourist visa with the intention of staying on for the purpose of earning a living. These women, without valid permits, are called illegal foreign workers. The second group includes political refugees, asylum seekers, and victims of global sex trafficking who seek work to sustain themselves. Most of these women have crossed the border illegally and are called infiltrators by the authorities.[1] A special, in-depth study of the second group involves factors that cannot be discussed in this context.

The focus of this chapter is on women defined as voluntary migrants, whose movement between countries takes place on a relatively free basis and who fall into the category of legitimate workers operating within the laws and statutes of a sovereign national state. Migrant workers from about ninety countries have come to work in Israel over the last two decades (Population and Immigration Authority data, 2012).[2] Among all the migrant women regarded as legal workers in Israel, in this chapter I take a close look at the Filipino community. Because in-depth research and knowledge of each and every community is virtually impossible, I have selected the largest and most visible community, which is also the most well established and diversified. The Filipino community is composed of women of diverse status and backgrounds who have migrated for various reasons. The artists discussed here represent merely a part of the whole picture, and my hope is that this will suffice to teach something about the community in general.

The artwork of migrant workers does not receive any significant exposure in the Israeli space; most of the exhibitions that have been realized were part of an initiative of the embassy of the artist's country of origin. In addition, some group exhibitions, such as photography competitions in the community, have been held under the aegis of the Tel Aviv municipality at municipal sites, such as the Einav Cultural Center. Exhibitions of art by migrants are seldom held at galleries, although one such exhibition was held at the Hanina Gallery in Tel Aviv. This was an exhibition of the Eritrean artist Fetsum Takalmariam titled "Works" in 2011.[3] To date, no exhibitions dedicated to gendered aspects of the art of migrant women, called foreign workers in prevalent terms, have been held in Israeli art institutions.

FEMALE MIGRANT WORKERS AROUND THE WORLD

Data regarding world migration in our current age of globalization indicates that an ever-growing number of people are in motion. In many countries no accurate data are available regarding migrants, and it is difficult to trace these trends systematically and across time. The fact that data collection systems differ from place to place also makes it difficult to make cross-national comparisons (Ehrenreich and Russell Hochschild, 2004: 5). According to World Bank data for 2010, out of 215 million people who reside outside their homeland, 48.4% are women—that is, more than 100 million are migrant women (World Bank, 2011: ix).

Despite the lack of precise data, a relatively clear trend is evident, as scholars concur that almost half of the world's migrant population is women. This has given rise to the concept of the "feminization of world migration" (Castles and Miller, 1993; Momsen, 2004). Nicola Piper, a sociologist researching migration movements, points to four phenomena that reflect these data and enable the improved monitoring and study of female migration: (1) greater statistical visibility, partly because of the view that female employment constitutes a separate sector; (2) a real numerical rise in the number of women in all forms of migration; (3) a dramatic increase in the number of men who cannot find full-time work in their homeland and rely on the income provided by their wives or other female family members, who look for work abroad; and (4) a growing demand for the types of jobs regarded as feminine in developed and developing countries (Piper, 2008: 2–3). The causes of female work migration are numerous. Among the prominent ones are economic incentives; the need to preserve family unity (in cases when the male spouse migrates before the rest of the family and they want to join him); the desire to escape difficult personal circumstances deriving from gender, religious, or ethnic violence; and the wish for a better personal future and higher education for one's children (DeLaet, 1999). The money that migrant workers send back to their homeland helps reduce their family's poverty, enabling them to invest in health insurance, education, and small businesses.

Interestingly, data concerning migration destinations indicate that what is known as south-south migration (i.e., migration from one developing country to another) is greater than south-north migration (i.e., migration from a developing country to one with a high income that belongs to the Organization for Economic Cooperation and Development

[OECD]) (Hujo and Piper, 2010).[4] This statistic contradicts the general prevalent assumption that the overwhelming majority of migrant workers move from poorer (south) to richer (north) countries in overall global movements (World Bank, 2011: ix). In fact, more than half of the world migration corridors are between developing countries.

More and more studies in recent decades have been dedicated to the subject of global female migration and its gender aspects. An important example is a collection of articles published under the title *Global Women: Nannies, Maids, and Sex Workers in the New Economy*, edited by Barbara Ehrenreich and Arlie Russell Hochschild (2004). This book contains a multifaceted discussion of the subject of female migrant workers. The editors call for an open, in-depth analysis of the situation of the millions of "transparent women" by perceiving them on their own terms, as "full human beings . . . strivers as well as victims, wives and mothers as well as workers—sisters, in other words, with whom we in the First World may someday define a common agenda" (51).

WORK MIGRATION TO ISRAEL

Work migration to Israel began after the Israeli occupation of the West Bank and Gaza Strip as a result of the Six Day War (1967), which gave Israelis the opportunity to use Palestinian workers who were seeking employment. Since the end of the 1970s, foreign workers from other countries have also arrived sporadically. These workers made up a largely limited, spontaneous, and illegal workforce until the 1980s (Sabar, 2008). At the end of the 1990s, after the outbreak of the First Intifada and limitations on the entry of Palestinian workers into Israel for security reasons, the Israeli government adopted a cautious policy of encouraging migrant workers from other countries, delimited by quota (Kemp and Raijman, 2008). After a decade of this policy, the number of foreign workers in Israel was estimated to be 240,000, constituting 9.4% of the workforce in the country (Central Bureau of Statistics press release, October 2003, cited in Kemp and Raijman, 2008: 10).

Apart from the need to replace Palestinian labor, the cabinet's decision to bring in foreign workers at the beginning of the 1990s was also due to the attempt on the part of the economic elites in Israel to liberalize the economy (Kemp and Raijman, 2008: 43–45). These interests, which, from the perspective of the economic logic that motivated them, were linked to the neoliberal trends of globalization, joined the local circumstances and logic of separation generated by the First Intifada that gained force after the Oslo Accords. This combination of political and economic factors is a striking example of the changes introduced in Israel by the transnational era, in which political agendas and economic changes that affect the global movement of people from place to place are manifested in Israel in a unique way. More than two decades after the beginning of the massive wave of global migrant workers into Israel, scholars of the phenomenon agree that the government's decision to invite foreign workers by quota and the processes it has generated have created a new and distinctive social category in Israel of noncitizens "living in the 'backyard' of Israeli society" (Kemp and Raijman, 2008: 11).

Two primary economic sectors in Israel use the services of female migrant workers. The first is home caregiving and privatized health services, a sector that emerged and developed locally only with the opening of the country to an international workforce. This subgroup is largely composed of Filipina and Nepalese women. The second sector consists of service workers—house and office cleaners, au pairs, and restaurant and catering service workers. This subgroup is primarily composed of African and Latin American migrant women. A low percentage of female migrant workers are also employed in the agricultural sector (Sabar, 2008: 39).

Although the numerical data regarding migrant workers in Israel indicate the large scope of the phenomenon, it is not totally accurate or reliable, with different sources giving divergent figures. According to data provided by the Immigration Authority for June 2012, there were 215,000 so-called foreign workers in Israel. The distribution among the various foreign workers (in the terminology used in the publication) is infiltrators (62,000), legal foreign workers (47, 000), illegal foreign workers (14,000), and tourists without valid visas (92,000). The overwhelming majority of the legal foreign workers (41,000 out of 47,000) are employed in the caregiving sector. A different source for this set of data derives from a prominent NGO known as Kav LaOved (Worker's Hotline), whose website gives a number closely corresponding to the official data published by the state: 180,000 migrant workers living and working in Israel. Despite the attempt to provide as broad and reliable account as possible, the status of migrant workers in Israel, based on concrete data, is nonlabile and constantly changing and is thus difficult to determine unambiguously. Because of the lack of fixed migration policy or legislation, the reality on the ground is largely shaped by temporary regulations, rulings, and decisions (frequently arbitrary and local) made by such bodies as the Interior Ministry. Many actors operate in the field, all of whom contribute to the permanent lack of stability and vagueness in the lives and reality of migrant women in Israel. Thus, for example, a meeting of the Knesset special committee set up to look into the "problem of foreign workers," as it was officially titled, at which the findings of a study of the subject were presented, was attended by representatives from over 18 bodies and organizations: manpower agencies, organizations for the elderly and disabled, caregiving and welfare agencies, human rights organizations, researchers from academia, the Ministry of Health, the National Insurance Institute, the Interior Ministry, the Finance Ministry, the Bank of Israel, the police force, the Population and Immigration Authority, the Ministry of Industry, Trade, and Employment, the Education Ministry, the Justice Ministry, and UN refugee commissioners—each pushing different and often contradicting agendas.[5]

In our current global reality the debate over the pros and cons of allowing work migration into a country has long become passé. Nation-states can only choose the most suitable migration policy that will channel migration into orderly, creative, and humanitarian channels and produce the greatest benefit for the migrants and their countries of birth and for the target countries and their citizens. Despite the high rate of migration, no comprehensive migration policy exists in Israel to date. In contrast to other countries in which religion does not constitute a central criterion for citizenship, Israel's status as a Jewish state precludes the assimilation and naturalization of non-Jewish immigrants. Over the years the government's migration policy has been consistent only in not granting citizenship to non-Jews. In every other sense its treatment of migrant workers has been neither uniform nor consistent.

This fact has been noted by activists working in the field and in academia, both groups bringing it to the attention of the public and the leaders of Israel's political parties. Thus, for example, jurists Shomo Avineri, Amnon Rubinstein, and Ruth Gavizon—three of the most influential figures in the Israeli justice system—submitted a report on the subject of migration policy to then-president Shimon Peres, Prime Minister Binyamin Netanyahu, Justice Minister Yaakov Neeman, and Interior Minister Eli Yishai in September 2009, in which they stated: "Israel has no modern migration legislature. Its institutions are not prepared to deal with the hundreds of thousands of migrants illegally resident in the country. The authorities' strategic thinking is deficient, there is no vision, and no goals or aims have been defined. . . . This leaves the field of the entry into the State as wild and unsupervised territory that lies in the hands of clerks and policemen whose decisions are made arbitrary and frequently implemented with brutality" (Hasson, 2009: 5).

As mentioned, Israel sustains a firm stance about non-Jewish migrants and does not allow any channel for their assimilation as citizens, systematically avoiding any official policy or legislation about it. Following a demand of the OECD from 2012 about this issue, the state responded, "There is no change in the Israeli government's policy. Migrant workers come to Israel for a brief and limited period. Their stay is thus designed to be temporary. Their arrival as migrant workers does not in and of itself constitute a track for future residency or citizenship" (*Ministry of Industry, Trade, and Labor Report to the OECD*, 2012).

In additional to the state's official statements, the verbal definitions prevalent in the public discourse and mass media with regard to non-Jewish migrant workers also reflect the discriminatory attitude toward them. As mentioned, they are called foreign workers, a term that limits their existence to the purpose for which they were brought into the country. The way in which they are related to is thus reduced to work, as though they are machines rather than human beings. In this sense, they constitute the ultimate Other: not part of the Jewish Israeli collective but merely tolerated as servants of the citizens. The term *foreign worker* thus signifies exclusion, social exploitation, invisibility, and marginalization. In the framework of this problematic reality, the workers' basic human rights are frequently violated. They are often forced into illegal binding employment arrangements and subject to degrading laws and procedures. Although this policy creates severe problems for male and female migrant workers alike, those faced by female migrant workers are particularly acute, especially in issues that relate to reproduction—pregnancy and childbirth—as the artists themselves will testify in this chapter.

Despite the limitations and complex situation caused by the lack of government policy with regard to comprehensive migration laws in Israel, some proactive action is being taken by the government. According to the 2012 report issued by the Ministry of Industry, Trade, and Labor, the government is now making an effort to prevent exploitative agency fees in light of the OECD's demands. These include bilateral agreements for mobilizing workers and the granting of priority to the implementation of these agreements in cooperation with the International Organization of Migrants (IOM). To date, such agreements have been signed with Thailand and Bulgaria, who have agreed to a quota of construction and agricultural workers whose working conditions will be supervised (*Ministry of Industry, Trade, and Labor Report to the OECD*, 2012). Because these jobs are essentially filled by men, the supervision of migrant women still leaves much to be desired.

As in many other cases in which the state does not take action—or does so in an inadequate manner—the gap is filled by local municipal authorities, NGOs, and civic bodies. In Israel several organizations have been established to protect migrant workers. These include the prominent NGO Kav LaOved, which seeks to protect foreign workers' rights. One of the first bodies to offer solutions to the problems and needs of migrant workers, whose actions have been the most important and effective to date, was the Tel Aviv municipality, under whose jurisdiction the largest group of migrant workers in Israel resides. In 1999 the municipality formed Mesila: The Aid and Information Center for foreign communities.[6] Together with help from private donors, Mesila provides information services, a response to emergency needs in situations of crisis, Hebrew classes, vocational courses, child and youth care, and activities for the community (Sabar, 2008: 41). The Tel Aviv municipality's work has even led to a quiet revolution in the field of education, with migrant children beginning to be absorbed into the municipal educational system starting in September 2001 (Kemp and Raijman, 2008: 181–82).

Such steps are consistent with existing trends in other countries. Big cities across the world are turning into global cities in which complex networks are created that enable migrant workers with no option to become citizens to take care of their needs and live in a community framework instead of being isolated and alienated, without any sense of community and support. As researcher Sasskia Sassen observes, although the large concentrations of migrant workers in big cities do not wield any official civic power, they have a strong presence (Sassen, 2004). Sassen asserts that it is important to find ways for citizenless migrant workers, with or without temporary permits, to become municipal citizens. In the context of world migration, the municipal space has won a special status and attitude, with cities across the world adopting the policy of being sanctuary cities. One such example is Chelsea, Massachusetts, whose city council declared in 2007 that "the City of Chelsea rejects the use of the word 'illegal' and 'alien' to describe any human being."[7]

The big metropolis that becomes a sanctuary city is a prominent feature of the liminal space in which migrant workers find themselves. Large cities cater to the migrant workers' need to find alternative, inclusive frameworks to replace the normative public space and civic institutions and social relations unavailable to them as noncitizens, because they are considered temporary Others.

In Israel the hundreds of thousands of migrant workers excluded from Israeli society, living on its margins as transparent women and men, can be conceptualized in relation to the framework of Western liberal discourse, which drives them outside its boundaries. Roy Wagner, a researcher of social science and an activist in the Kav LaOved organization, in his discourse analysis of the Western liberal political climate, defines the place and status of female migrant workers through negation and exclusions. The basic discursive positions, or categories, he considers are economic agent, mother, victim, and citizen. As he observes, migrant workers do not encompass any of these four categories (Wagner, 2010).

In this chapter I use Wagner's analysis. In meetings I conducted with the migrant artists whose work is discussed here, the women gave striking examples of various forms of exclusion: violations of basic workers' rights (e.g., nonpayment for extra hours, discriminatory treatment of pregnant women, illegal binding agreements for employment, agency fees above the legal amount) and violations of their rights as human beings (e.g., sexist and racist attitudes that create in them a deep and pervading sense of loneliness and isolation).

FILIPINA MIGRANT WORKERS IN ISRAEL

A large, well-established, and vibrant community of Filipina migrant workers exists in Israel, and it operates a plethora of social, cultural, religious, educational, and recreational activities. However, in contrast to the multidimensional, rounded subjects they are, in the popular discourse in Israel the epithet "Filipina" has become a generic word for "caregiver"; the statement "Either we get a Filipina or we put grandma into a home" is commonplace. According to data from the Israeli Population and Immigration Authority, as of the end of 2012, of the 35,000 female migrant workers considered legal in Israel, 34,000 were employed in the caregiving sector. On the basis of division according to country of origin, the Filipino community is the largest migrant group in the country and in the care-giving sector alike. Of the 15,000 Filipinas in Israel, 12,000 are employed in the caregiving sector (data from the Population and Immigration Authority, 2012).[8]

The export of workers is an important economic sector in the Philippines, a country defined as a developing nation. In 2010 the Philippines was fourth on the list of countries in which money is transferred to the state from workers abroad—$21.3 billion, about 12% of GDP for 2009 (World Bank, 2011: 13).[9] The Philippines thus forms a kind of superpower in exporting workers; the official estimate from the end of 2007 indicates that 8.73 million Filipinos (out of a total population of 88 million, according to the Central Bureau of Statistics) reside outside the country, of whom 5 million are defined as "overseas Filipino workers" or temporary migrant workers.[10] In 2008, for example, 1.24 million Filipinos left the country, or 3,400 daily.[11]

One explanation for this phenomenon relates to the high rate of unemployment in the Philippines. The export of workers may also stem, however, from additional internal political factors. Thus, for example, many of the artists with whom I spoke observed that the corruption and nepotism that are rampant in the Philippines make it difficult for those without connections to find steady jobs. These features are characteristic of the Marcos regime to the present government, which has yet to show any signs of being capable of dealing with them. According to the world corruption index issued by Transparency International (an NGO dedicated to promoting a noncorrupt world), out of 176 nations in 2012, the Philippines was 105th, with an index of 34 (highest place indicating the most corrupted country) (Transparency International, 2012). These data demonstrate, even if partly, why the migrant Filipina community in Israel is so large and well established.

The community of Filipina workers in Israel has a rich cultural basis that includes newspapers, various interest groups based on special hobbies such as photography societies, basketball teams, and community events related to Philippines national holidays. Despite its marginalization from general civic life, Filipina migrants have a relatively strong community infrastructure in relation to other migrant communities in Israel, such as Chinese or Nepalese migrants. Unfortunately, this does not preclude its members from being affected by exclusion and the problems related to their status as foreign workers.

The profile of the Filipina migrant worker in Israel is of a young and educated woman, arriving from either a rural or an urban area. Some of the women are single, and others are married and have children, mostly living apart from them and being raised in the Philippines by other family members. In contrast to the women artists discussed in the previous chapters of this book, I do not note the date of birth of the Filipina women artists discussed here. In general, the women are in their 20s to 40s; most possess a valid working permit, but some do not have a clear legal status. All the interviewees preferred that I publish minimal formal information about them, apart from their names. Because of a narrative of humiliation and sexual exploitation experienced by one interviewee, her story is told without any identifying name.

The artworks of the women presented in this chapter help us to understand that they are not merely workers or foreigners but subjects—daughters, sisters, wives, and mothers—who have left an entire world behind them to provide for their loved ones and better their own lives. Their artwork highlights all the exclusions from which they suffer and with which they must deal: income and dilemmas related to motherhood, legal status, and community belonging. For this reason, their own voices and perspective are put forth, in their own words, so that they can be heard.

EMPLOYMENT

Marylou Sulit Muga is a caregiver for a young Israeli woman with physical disabilities. Her photograph *She Works Hard for the Money* (2012) embodies her sense of responsibility and need to sustain her extended family, left behind in the Philippines (Figure 27). The photo shows a pile of various monetary bills—Israeli shekels, American dollars, and Philippine pesos—that constitute the reason Muga is in Israel and the forces that have motivated her to leave her family. The composition forms a sort of

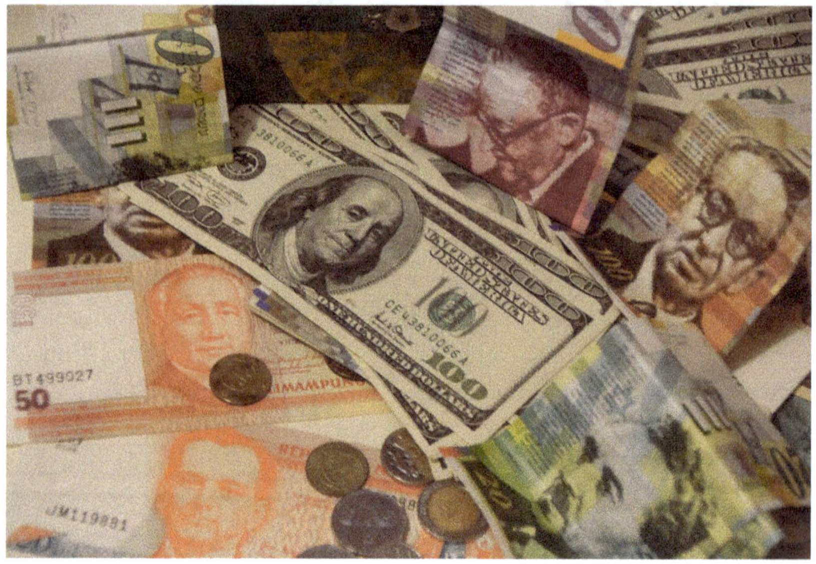

FIGURE 27. Marylou Sulit Muga, *She Works Hard for the Money*, 2012. Color photo.

financial world map. The Philippine pesos lie at the bottom, forming the base for all the monetary actions. At the center lie the American dollars, the currency of the political, economic, and cultural superpower. The Israeli shekels are arranged as a flowered framework around and above—folded and scattered like leaves fluttering in the wind. In this photo the capitalist system is encapsulated, accurately describing the forces that frame the artist's life.

In addition to her job as a caregiver, Muga is a column writer and editor for *Manila Tel Aviv* magazine a journal published in Israel for the Filipino community. In the Philippines Muga was an art teacher for thirteen years, until economic circumstances forced her to seek work in Israel, leaving her husband, children, and extended family behind. In an email exchange conducted after our interview, she told me why she chose photography as her primary art form.

> Photography helps me value the beauty in the nature around us, the beauty of all people. For me, in a certain sense, it helps preserve the art I used to create back home (mainly painting, but that is too time

> consuming, and I can't afford a studio here). I really long for the art activity I used to do. Today, photography and my journalistic writing fill almost every aspect of my free time. They ease my problems and exhaustion. . . . In my opinion, everyone in the world has a special talent and we all have to benefit from these. (Muga, personal correspondence, 2012)

Muga's camera lens also captures the daily life of Filipina migrant workers in Israel, including moments of difficulty and frustration as well as joy and celebration, such as church events, sightseeing trips, and recreational moments with friends from the community. In an extended series of photographs, Muga takes pains to present Filipinas as whole, round subjects, acting in a variety of ordinary human states—on their free day walking in public spaces, shopping, or keeping in contact with their family back in the Philippines.

Balancing work, domestic responsibilities, and recreation time is an especially important aspect of middle- and upper-class women's lives in Western countries. Apart from the help necessary to take care of ill or disabled family members—a task frequently filled by a paid caregiver—a relatively new trend exists in the West toward shifting caregiving and emotional responsibilities in the domestic sphere from women from Europe or America to non-Western women from developing countries. This reflects the unequal power relations between women around the world. Western women outsource domestic help, in most cases paying women from developing countries to take care of their homes while they develop their careers and invest in their fields of interest and self-achievement. Because Western values promote careers—housekeeping and childbearing do not fall into this category—economically strong women have the luxury of giving the task of caring for their children to other women. In turn, the caregivers have left their own children in the care of others—frequently grandmothers, aunts, sisters, or older daughters—in order to seek employment that will ensure their survival.

Researcher Arlie Russell Hochschild calls this phenomenon "emotional imperialism" and argues that Westerners regard female migrant workers as naturally graced with emotional talents especially suitable for caregiving, because they are more tolerant and loving than Western women (Russell Hochschild, 2004: 39–40). They think of themselves as less tolerant with a more limited ability to give love because they are career- and self-fulfillment-oriented, striving to liberate themselves from the emotional and time-consuming responsibilities of caring for others. Because of their privileged position, they can simply import these qualities from the East or elsewhere in the world. As Russell Hochschild observes, Western imperialism, which reached its height in the eighteenth and nineteenth centuries and exhausted natural resources (oil, gold, and diamonds) as much as human resources, has thus been resurrected in the form of the globalized exploitation of caregiving resources, emotional fostering, and love. Current stances of feminist criticism maintain that the Western feminist movement that worked to free women from traditional gender roles, such as homemaking and child raising, has in effect promoted the oppression of non-Western women who undertake these traditional roles for them.

Marylou Muga, for example, told me that she constantly hears about employers who do not treat caregivers properly: "Israeli employers frequently think that we, the caregivers, are stupid and uneducated. What they don't know is that education is the most important thing for Filipinos. Many of us have academic degrees in all sorts of desired professions. I, for example, have a BEd in Art and an MBS. In many instances, the Israeli employer himself doesn't have a university education but assumes that his caregiver is ignorant and has to have basic things explained to her" (Muga, personal correspondence, 2012). The degrading attitude of Israelis toward Filipinas—not appreciating their education or life experiences or their agency and treating them as functional objects—is well represented in the four categories conceptualized by Roy Wagner mentioned earlier. The first exclusion within the framework of the liberal discourse is that of being an economic agent. As Wagner observes, economic agents are those who can choose the job in which they are employed in an act of rational, free choice and in accordance with their talents. If a person is prevented from making such a choice because of coercion, power disparities, knowledge gaps, or irrational traditions, that individual is not an economic agent (Wagner, 2010: 66). Marylou Muga left her life and country to earn money through work that is not her true profession. Some would say that she chose to do this in order to break through the boundaries imposed on her and improve her family circumstances. Others would say that this act was forced on her by economic reality, family constraints, or deliberate policy on the part of the regime in the Philippines and in light of global economics.

All these reasons and concepts belong to the Western liberal economic discourse, however; notions of free will and rational choice might be irrelevant in the Filipina migrant's context. As Wagner explains, "The vocabulary required to describe their decision to leave and work in another country (as well as many other decisions in a variety of contexts) is not compatible with the distinction between an action forced upon an individual, on the one hand, and an individual free to choose, on the other. This decision does not pertain to an autonomous individual" (Wagner, 2010: 67). Significantly, although the migrant workers are not economic agents, they nonetheless play an important role in the economic field—as economic objects, by paying thousands of dollars to mediators and manpower agencies to bring them to Israel and by transferring a steady stream of foreign currency back to the Philippines. In 2011, for example, Filipina migrant workers contributed $21.3 billion to the Philippine economy, 12% of its GDP (World Bank, 2011: 13–14). They thus serve as active economic objects on whom the Philippine economy is heavily dependent.

CLASS AND SEXUAL HARASSMENT

At the juncture between economic and artistic value stand the works of Marita Reyes, also employed in Israel as a caregiver. Reyes makes sculptured objects, such as the two swans that form the subject of a work from 2010 (Figure 28). The swans—and other objects, such as colorful jars (Figure 29) and animals such as birds, hares, and cats—are made using origami-like techniques prevalent in the Filipina community. Filipinas learn this technique from one another, sometimes while still living in the Philippines and sometimes after they come to Israel. Most of the women who create the objects work as caregivers, using their spare time on the job (such as when the elderly or disabled individuals they look after are resting) rather than their free time during the weekends, when they gather with friends and family from the community. As Reyes observes, "You know. I'm tired almost all the time. The grandfather is heavy and he can't do anything on his own. When he sleeps, I rest, but sometimes I get bored. So then I make these paper things" (Reyes, interview by author, 2010).

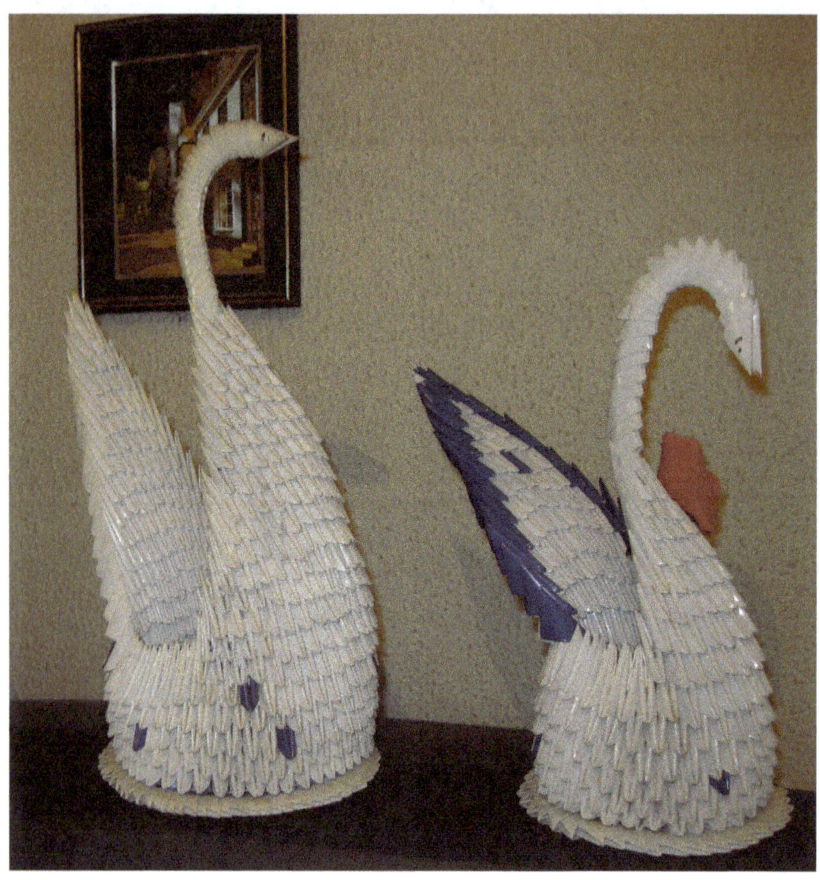

FIGURE 28. Marita Reyes, Untitled, 2010. Mixed media.

Cultural researcher Shoshana-Rose Marzel writes about female handicraft in marginalized communities in Israel, describing the context in which pieces of the type are created: "Although the handwork of migrant workers has a vast array of sources of inspiration, the number of works they produce is very limited. This is not surprising—all their energies go into work, most of them not having any time or mental respite to engage in handicrafts. Some of them, however, break this mold and engage in handicraft—for example, Filipinas who create origami works" (Marzel, 2008: 85). According to Marzel, the feature common to all the female artists in marginal communities in Israel, including Filipina

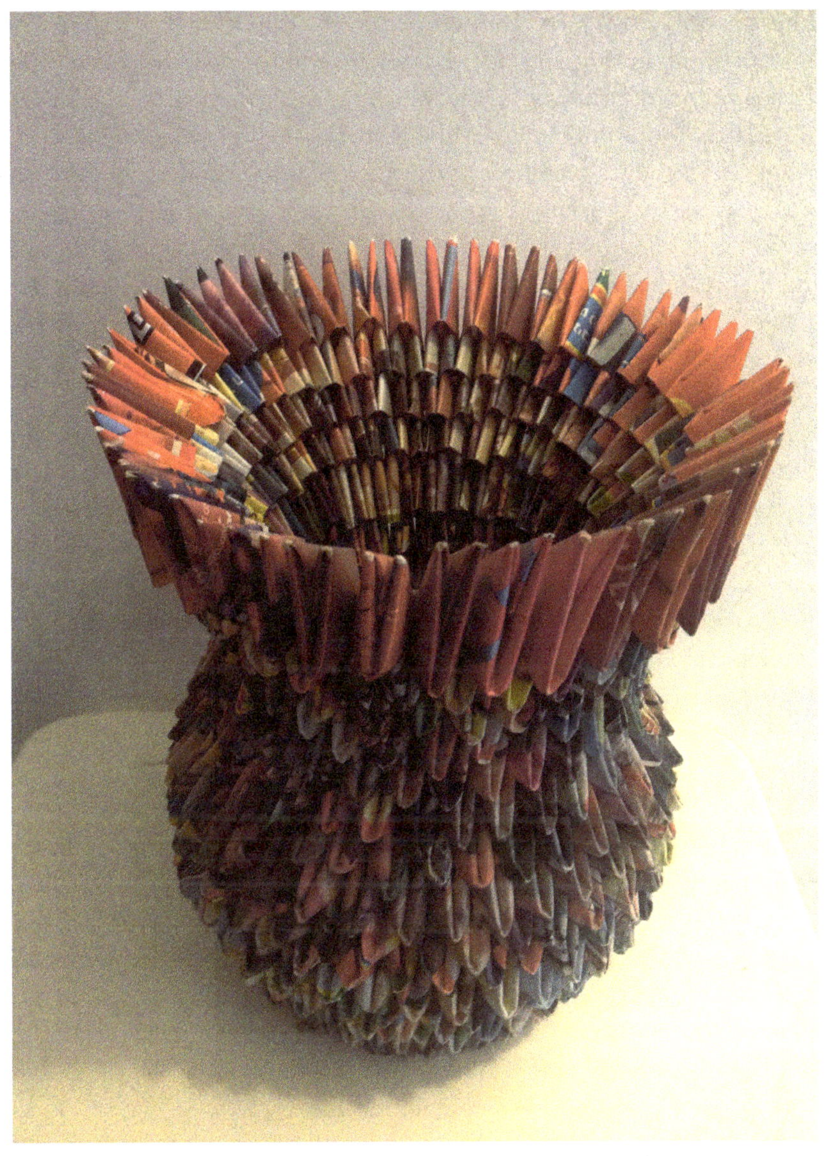

FIGURE 29. Marita Reyes, Untitled, 2010. Mixed media.

migrant workers, is their ability to create objects from the simplest of materials: "It is primarily creativity born out of the poverty of materials. Even in times of real distress, the woman finds a way to create. . . . Sometimes, these works turn into a means that can grant the woman empowerment, at times even economic independence" (85). Although Reyes does not create jars and paper sculptures to sell as a way of supplementing her income, she notes that she finds great satisfaction from her art, alongside another reason: "I don't want to think a lot. I think about my children at home, I miss them, so instead I make swans. It's better that way" (Reyes, interview by author, 2010).

To work in Israel, Reyes left her husband, three children, and extended family in the Philippines. In our meetings she told me that she has been in Israel for nine years, during which time she has not been back home once. She regularly sends a monthly sum to her family so that they can achieve a better quality of life and future, in particular to ensure that the children gain a higher education, which is costly in the Philippines. Reyes repeatedly stresses that she would have preferred to remain in the Philippines and find a job there; she certainly would not have chosen to come to Israel. Using the analysis offered by Roy Wagner, the concepts of choice or necessity are beyond her horizon, ensconced in the Western liberal discourse.

Although it is important to conceptualize Reyes's situation in alternative terms, her particular situation may, in relative terms, be better than that of other Filipinas in Israel. Employed for many years by a nice, honest, and respecting family, she does not have to worry about losing her work permit. This means that she is able to access the public sphere and walk the streets freely, unafraid of being caught and deported by the immigration authorities. Filipina caregivers are particularly vulnerable in this regard, as they are given work permits for a specific employer. If they wish or are forced to leave that employer for any reason—withheld pay, sexual harassment, or simply the death of the elderly person they have been serving—they immediately become subject to deportation. To forestall this dire circumstance, Filipina migrant workers must independently find a new employer within a limited time period—a daunting task at the best of times and one that is compounded by the Filipinas not speaking the language and possessing few connections with veteran citizens who might need their services. When they do not have a permit, caregivers tend to stay indoors as much as possible, fearing being caught by the immigration police who patrol the streets.

As sociologists Kemp and Raijman observe, policing of the mobility in space is a striking feature of the exclusion that migrant workers suffer: "It is no coincidence that, together with the globalization of the demand for a cheap work force embodied in migrant workers, the rights of these workers to mobility have become a scarcer than ever resource and a primary stratified mechanism between different social groups" (2008: 13).

In 2006 the Israeli Supreme Court ruled that binding agreements on migrant workers were illegal and went so far as to call them a form of modern slavery. To date, however, no proper alternative arrangement has been instituted. On the ground, rulings allow de facto bondage (Amendment to the Law of Entry into Israel, 2011), and the "corporate agreement" that permits the employment of migrant workers through manpower agencies is extremely problematic (Goffstein, 2013: 386). The picture is one of a fluid, unstable reality; the level of bondage and restriction of such workers is difficult to determine, with each migrant worker's experience or situation being different from that of the next. A great vagueness pervades the subject, as it also does in numerous other aspects of female migrant workers' lives and status in Israel.

The exclusion from economic agency is bound up with gross class exploitation, for example, the withholding of pay and abominable working conditions. This in turn frequently leads to physical, mental, and at times sexual exploitation and assault. Women who work in homes and live at their workplace, who take care of elderly people, people with disabilities, or children, or who work as housekeepers and cleaners are particularly vulnerable to such abuse. As early as 2004, a World Bank report recognized that migrant women's work in homes, together with male work in construction and agriculture, entails especially high risks as a result of their isolation and the high frequency of exploitation, exclusion, deprivation, and neglect (ILO, 2004).

Unfortunately, many employers are convinced that the caregiving workers in their homes come on an "all-included" basis. Examples abound of the slippery slope that leads from economic and class exploitation to physical and mental abuse. An anonymous artist chose to tell me in confidentiality about her experiences. The elderly woman she was looking after treated her as her inferior. When they went out on errands, the employer would overload her with heavy goods and carrier bags. She refused to buy her a refreshing drink, and when the caregiver asked her, "Why, grandmother? Are you so poor that you can't buy me a soft drink from a kiosk?" she replied, "How dare you talk to me like that! Remember, I'm not your friend. You work for me." What upset the caregiver was the fact that "she doesn't understand that I'm a human being too. She thinks she's a human being and I'm 'only a worker'—like a machine or robot" (interview by author, 2012). This migrant worker had been in Israel just over a year, and during her first period of residence with this employer she encountered numerous difficulties. One of the central issues was food. Her employer refused to understand that she was not used to the local food, frequently "forgot" to buy rice for her, and told her she could eat bread and hummus, like her. On several occasions, the caregiver went to bed on an empty stomach.

Moreover, as the caregiver also explained, her being a woman entailed special difficulties. Migrant women, she said, have different experiences from migrant men: "Women feel deeper emotions; men don't need deep and ongoing emotional satisfaction. Men only want to work and eat. Women want love and share and they are very disappointed when their emotional lives are not full" (interview by author, 2012). She then went on to speak of the feeling of gender vulnerability women have in the public sphere. She did not always feel safe going back to the flat in southern Tel Aviv that she shares with friends on the weekend or walking through the streets around the central bus station—an area known for its poverty, prostitution, and drug usage—because men would approach her in dark alleys.

An even more painful subject for Filipinas is the danger of sexual assault that might happen at the workplace. While looking for another job on the weekends, this anonymous interviewee was referred to an elderly man who was confined to a wheelchair. The first opportunity they were alone, he tried to persuade her to sit on his lap and caress him, even declaring that he would be willing to pay her extra for that. Although she got up and left immediately, she did nothing further about it; she did not tell anyone because of her shame and did not file a police report for fear of becoming known to the authorities.

Organizations such as Kav LaOved are familiar with many such stories of sexual harassment, a problem that women caregivers who live in their employers' homes are particularly exposed to (Goffstein, 2013: 388–89). Three Israeli coordinators of Kav LaOved described the phenomenon in a text published on the Haokets website: "Many women migrant workers who come to Kav LaOved's offices to get help in exercising their working rights and more than often also tell stories of employers that perform various forms of sexual exploitation" (Leibowitz et al., 2013). Sometimes the person being cared for is the abuser; at others times the abuse is meted out by one of the employer's family members. Evidence of such cases is accumulating, less with the police than with Kav LaOved.

In addition to the reality of living in a patriarchal society, which is a priori disinclined to believe women's complaints of sexual assault, one of the greatest problems for female migrant workers is credibility. Frequently, they encounter a lack of belief and cooperation on the part of the police and official institutions when they try to file a complaint. This circumstance is compounded by the fact that they do not always know to whom they can turn to complain or have enough knowledge of Hebrew to adequately or accurately express themselves. Most significant of all, they feel alone and isolated, and their lack of family or supportive community dissuades them from embarking on the complex process of filing a complaint. Statistics indicate that female migrant workers who have been sexually assaulted prefer not to make complaints, choosing rather to focus on exercising their economic rights and on keeping their work and residency visas valid (Porat, 2013).

The police and Immigration Authorities in Israel do not sufficiently punish employers who abuse their female workers or extort them. The Immigration Bureau, an arm of the Interior Ministry, replaced the Ministry of Industry and Trade in 2009 as the government body responsible for the employment of foreign workers. Since it has been in charge, complaints filed against employers have not been pursued with the same intensity as in the years before the transfer from the Ministry of Industry and Trade (Weiler-Polak, 2011: 7).

This degrading, inhumane treatment reflects the discursive exclusion category of being a nonvictim (Wagner, 2010). In the legal framework of Israeli laws and in accordance with the liberal political discourse, a female migrant worker cannot be conceptualized as a victim because that notion does not apply to migrant workers (Wagner, 2010: 70). Even after international pressure led Israel to recognize those who have fallen victim to human trafficking, the government has continued to ignore the rights of "regular" migrant women, such as caregivers, and has made no effort to enforce rules that can protect them. Although not the victims of trafficking, migrant women are frequently the target of crimes, such as rape and sexual exploitation, and are subject to starvation, slavery and forced bondage, embezzlement, and violation of their basic human rights—and they receive no help from state systems. Therefore, asserts Wagner, under the logic of the liberal discourse, a female migrant worker in Israel cannot be recognized as the victim of a crime. She is thus left doubly defenseless, a victim of working laws and of personal laws equally.

MOTHERS AND THE DEPORTATION OF CHILDREN

The state imposes another severe form of exclusion on female migrant workers in Israel by violating their right to become mothers, giving them an ultimatum: motherhood or work. According to Western liberal thought, mothers are regarded as immobile objects that remain fixed in one place while taking care of their families (Wagner, 2010). In contrast, migrant workers are considered temporary objects, uprooted and away from their natural place. They are thus considered to possess no possibility of raising a family while away from their home. In other words, their temporary status leads to the breaking of the linkage between migrant working and motherhood (Wagner, 2010: 68).

In Israel this exclusion is strikingly exemplified in the legal procedure called "Procedure for Dealing with Pregnant Foreign Workers." This gives the state the right to expel migrant workers who have borne a child. Following the amendment of this regulation—the result of vigorous activity of Israeli human rights and politicians—female migrant workers can now leave Israel with their children and return to work without them.[12] Although clearly still not satisfying, this amendment was a great achievement in and of itself, involving much strenuous lobbying.

In Israel the motherhood of migrant workers is subject to a doubly hypocritical attitude. On the one hand, Israelis are patronizingly astonished that the women have left their children behind and gone to another country to work; on the other hand, the proscription and expulsion of pregnant women and mothers who seek to live together with their children and closely supervise their education and well-being expose the fact that officials have no real interest in the fate of these women and children. Artist and caregiver Marylou Sulit Muga describes the common Israeli eye that looks and judges women migrant workers who are mothers.

> It is hard for Israelis to understand how I live far away from my family, working in a job in another country. My life always seems indecipherable in the eyes of Israelis, and they often ask me lots of questions. Once I was in a shopping mall with my employer and someone turned to me and said that my life is a disaster and asked me lots of questions, such as "How can you live without your children, without your husband?" . . . On the same occasion, a young Orthodox lad who heard the conversation was upset and said, "What, you've left your children? You don't love them?" Finally, he adamantly pronounced, "My mother would never do such a thing. She would never leave me and abandon me in such a way." Should I have had to answer and explain to this boy that by going away to work in Israel, I was giving my children a safer and brighter future, giving them the ultimate maternal gift? (Muga, interview by author, 2012)

In the Philippines, mothers who leave to work outside the country are a common phenomenon, often creating what Rachel Salazar Parreñas (2004) calls a "care crisis"—the splitting up of nuclear families, with the children thus growing up in alternative family arrangements. Female migrant workers are never fully integrated into the recipient society and cannot take their families with them to the host country. Nor can they visit their families regularly, as some workers do not earn sufficient money to travel back and forth. In contrast to the caregivers, those who receive the full care services—that is, Israeli citizens—benefit from this situation, receiving the undivided, daily attention they require from Filipina caregivers, whose own families are facing a maternal absence.

In the public discourse in Israel, some seek to demonize mothers that do live with their children in Israel, creating the impression that they are many in number and constitute a significant demographic hazard and threat to the homogeneity of the society. The public focus on the migrant mothers' otherness and differentiation of race and religion, using a racist mechanism, gains force from the idea of the need to maintain the majority of the Jewish population and the purity of its race. This racist discourse is loaded with a special gendered aspect, directed as it is particularly toward women. As scholars Yehuda Shenhav and Yossi Yonah observe, "The family, sexuality, and the nature of the woman are made objects of biopolitics, whose goal is the molding and establishment of the moral level of the white race" (2008: 22). Scholars Sigal Gooldin and Adriana Kemp similarly argue that the foreign, fertile body of the women migrant worker in Israel is

> at one and same time an object of the ethno-national discourse—which determines her foreign body to be an object for racification and a threat to the national collective—and the liberal discourse—which facilitates the deracialization of her foreign body by its positioning in the world of workforce and employment. The fertile body of the woman migrant worker thus becomes a political site that dialectically shifts as a movable object between migration laws and work laws, between racialization and deracialization. (Gooldin and Kemp, 2008: 260)

From the state's perspective, the migrant woman's fertile body must be controlled—monitored and managed in a way that "demands maneuvering between the conflicting worlds of the political economy of the workforce field and the political economy of symbolic relations with foreigners" (Gooldin and Kemp, 2008: 260). This fusion of perspectives—the laws of migration and the laws of employment—as applied to female migrant workers reflects the intersection of the categories of race, class, religion, and gender and their oppressive dimensions.

In 2009 the State of Israel determined to expel, for the first time, 1,200 children of migrant workers who had been born and brought up in the country. Up until that year, children of migrants had possessed no legal status, but an unwritten policy existed in which neither they nor their mothers were to be expelled (in contrast to fathers, who are expelled on a regular basis). In response to this cabinet decision, the organization Israeli Children was set up, and it initiated a series of demonstrations and organized media and lobbying campaigns related to the issue. Artist Sharon Miguel, a migrant worker who has two children who were born in Israel, took part in some of the organization's actions. In May 2010 Israeli Children held a demonstration against an upcoming expulsion in which

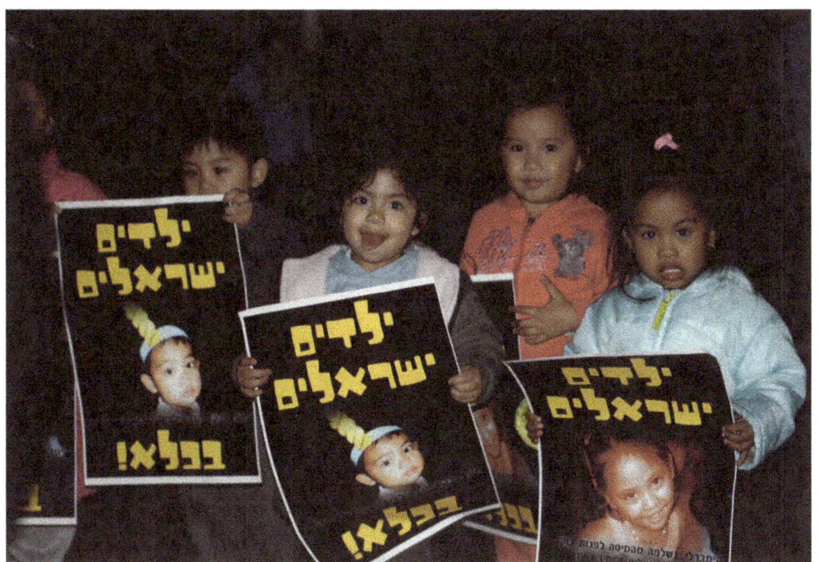

FIGURE 30. Sharon Miguel, Untitled, 2010. Color photo.

8,000 protesters participated, including politicians from across the political spectrum, ordinary Israeli citizens, and migrant men, women, and children from various countries. During the event, Miguel photographed several of the mothers and children under threat of expulsion (Figure 30). The photograph shows some of the children who participated in the demonstration holding photos of those who had been arrested by the authorities and expelled. This created the effect of a *mise en abyme*—an image of an image within another—thus strengthening and heightening the feeling of a dead-end. The children seem caught between two mirrors and do not have the means with which to break free from the trap. The photo expresses the fear and feeling of helplessness of children who regard Israel as their state, because they were born there, but are under threat of being expelled to a country they have never been to.

The issue of these Israeli-born children created a public storm in Israeli society, as politicians, journalists, social activists, and ordinary citizens participated in the public discussion it sparked. The question of expulsion turned into a basic moral question that refused to die down. The high-profile public activities of Israeli Children ensured that the migrant workers and their children, who up until then had been an invisible community living on the margins of Israeli society, became a visible population with a presence on the public agenda. Migrant workers and Israeli citizens fought side by side for social justice for children born in the country, seeking to guarantee their right to become part of Israeli society despite not being Jewish and being born to "foreign workers" residing "temporarily" in the country. Following a long and winding saga, it was decided to expel only 400 of the 1,200. Here, too, however, vagueness, lack of decisiveness, and inconsistency reign, and, to date, only a few of the 400 have actually been expelled. The process of granting permanent residency to the other 800 children who are eligible for citizenship similarly remains slow.

INVOLVEMENT AND EXCLUSION

Artist Esther Socalo is an example of a migrant worker whose motherhood is a continuous source of stress because she lives under the constant fear of being arrested by the immigration police and deported with her children. A dentist by profession, she could not find work in her field in the Philippines, so she came to Israel to work as a caregiver. Following the birth of her oldest child, she lost her work permit and was forced into working as a cleaner. After a decade in Israel, her identity has become multilayered, blending together the many facets of her life. Aspects of her homeland and her new country are reflected all at once: She speaks both Hebrew and Tagalog, celebrates both Passover and Easter, enjoys Israeli as much as Filipino food, and is raising a new family in Israel while maintaining connections with her family in the Philippines.

Socalo observes that as a female migrant worker, she faces unique gender problems. Male migrant workers are more frequently expelled, but many women like her are left single mothers. For some years she has been the sole breadwinner in the family, raising her first child alone.

> Before I became a mother, as a single woman in Israel, I was relatively free. I could work during the day and meet friends or rest and gather my forces in the evenings. The moment I had my daughter, I couldn't go out in the evenings at all, because I had to look after my child. My parents and sisters aren't here. Even today, every day I work in clean-

> ing, and in the afternoon I go home and get my two children from their educational framework. When they were very little, I didn't go out again until the next day, because I had to look after them. I feel completely exhausted and worn out. Every day, all I do is work and sleep, work and sleep—that's my life. (Socalo, interview by author, 2012)

To my question whether she would choose to come to Israel again if she knew the challenges she would have to face, she replied:

> No, of course not. I'm always in tension. When the kids were babies, I was always scared of the police, as though we're criminals. They've already burst into my apartment several times as though on a military operation. I was so afraid that I almost lost my mind. They cut off the electricity in the building minutes before they burst in so that we would be disoriented and not be able to escape, and then they broke down the door and blinded us with their flashlights. My daughter was only three months old. Since then I've been traumatized. When I go out onto the street, I'm always looking to see where the police could be under cover. For years I've lived like that, in fear. (Socalo, interview by author, 2012)

Despite the lack of security, Socalo is unsure whether she wants to return to the Philippines: "I can't go back and I can't really stay." The reason for her dilemma is that her son and daughter, both of whom were born and educated in Israel, see themselves as totally Israeli. This is especially true for her eldest, who has frequent discussions about leaving or staying in the only country she knows. Socalo thus feels that Israel is the only place for her to live, but although she applied for citizenship, the state denied it. Since then, she has applied again, and the small family is awaiting an answer from the state.

Despite her complex and unstable situation—or perhaps because it—Socalo conceptualizes her liminal and hybrid status in Israel through the lens of her camera. Having taken introductory and advanced photography courses given by the Mesila organization in Tel Aviv, her artwork reflects the way she perceives her position in Israeli society and her in-depth and intimate acquaintance with the Israeli space in which she lives. In a photograph from 2012 she depicts her own long shadow as it falls

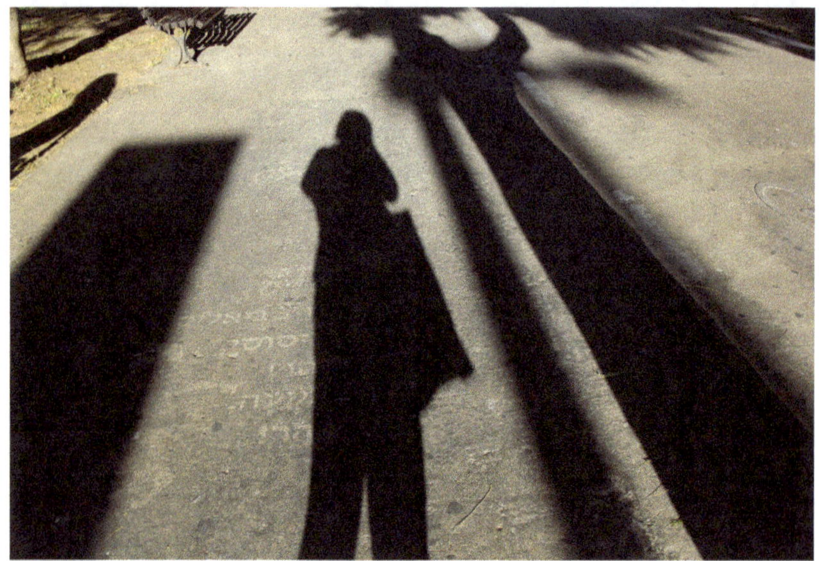

FIGURE 31. Esther Socalo, Untitled, 2012. Color photo.

on the pavement along the prestigious, upper-class Rothschild Boulevard in Tel Aviv. The shadow frames the words inscribed on the pavement—a quote from the famous children's song "Horseman" by the Jewish Israeli national poet, Hayim Nahman Bialik ("Run, little pony, run and gallop!") (Figure 31). The blending of the poet's words engraved on Rothschild Boulevard—the haven of bourgeois businesses and leisure activities in Tel Aviv—and the shadow of the migrant worker is a sophisticated tool Socalo uses to convey her situation and social status as a migrant worker in Israel. As she explains: "I chose to give you this photo because the shadow is like a symbol representing my status here in this country. It's like my unclear situation. Although I have family here, in a democratic country, the State doesn't recognize the status of children born here, and we do not count. They want us to be like a passing shadow" (Socalo, personal correspondence, 2012).

The symbolic meanings of status (citizen vs. noncitizen) and culture (Filipino vs. Israeli) produced in Socalo's photo reflect a grim, realistic reality accompanied by heavy irony. The permanent citizens residing on this prestigious Tel Aviv boulevard are accustomed to stepping and trampling on the words of the national poet—an act regarded as acceptable to those who "own" that cultural asset. The migrant worker only walks it as a shadow—a woman with no right to a real, physical body that can step on words that symbolize white, hegemonic Israeli culture. The shadow is an amorphous, elusive entity that engenders a double logic. On the one hand, the shadow, like the migrant woman worker, does not really exist; it is only a fleeting silhouette, a mere pale reflection. On the other hand, she is a threat, casting a dark shadow, both metaphorically and literally—a frightening and indecipherable stain on white, canonic Israeli society.

In the photograph, Socalo exercises stratified gaze relations. She presents herself both as she sees herself through her own eyes, conveying her experience of life in Israel, and as she is seen through the eyes of Israeli citizens. A dissonance exists between the way she feels toward local society and her place within it and the way in which others perceive her. Socalo takes a deep sense of involvement and interest in local events; her Facebook page addresses daily affairs in Israeli politics, and her posts on national stories, such as the discovery of the Dead Sea Scrolls or Gilad Shalit's captivity and release, change frequently. During our interview, Socalo expressed her feelings freely, saying that she found it interesting to meet and talk with me, but she also gave voice to her frustration on several occasions during the meeting, remarking with a grin, "I didn't really want to meet with you. I've already been interviewed so many times by Israeli women who are activists and such, but nothing comes out of it for me. Nothing ever changes. My situation stays the same. . . . In any case, you don't have any way of imagining or understanding my situation. You're not in my place. You'll never understand" (Socalo, interview by author, 2012). Her "place" is that of a migrant who, in her country of origin, pursued a prestigious profession as a dentist but was forced to uproot herself from her homeland and find work in Israel as a caregiver and then as a cleaner. She has given birth to two wonderful children but has to cope with bringing them up under split identities. Her civic status is unclear, and if she is deported, she does not know where she would go. Her children feel Israeli and, if expelled, have no other country they can truly call their own.

Her claim, expressed in artistic ways in her photographs, that Israelis cannot imagine or understand her situation, reflects yet another of the exclusions Roy Wagner identifies: the right to take part in civic praxis and freely engage in community involvement (Wagner, 2010: 73). Because they are evidently not citizens of the country in which they seek work, migrant workers are also denied the possibility of any civic organization, limiting even their basic rights of freedom of movement and expression. Many Filipina caregivers are allowed to leave their place of employment only on their day off; the rest of the week they are confined to their employer's house. They can be stopped at any time for routine checks by immigration police—carried out on the basis of profiling—to see if their permits are valid, risking immediate arrest and expulsion if not. Those who seek to become activists and contribute to their community, organizing demonstrations or any other activities to gain better working conditions and wages, become known to the authorities as initiators of community civil action and are thus at even greater risk; such political action on the part of migrant workers is met with hostility and at times even with persecution, arrest, and deportation (Wagner, 2010: 74).

Exclusion from the right to citizenship indicates the extent to which the status of women migrant workers within the framework of a host nation-state is unstable and liminal. As Wagner notes:

> Even the "International Convention on the Protection of the Rights of All Migrant Workers and Members of Their Families," which promises migrant workers and their families the shared platform of basic human rights, [is] so progressive that not a single developed country has dared sign it, [and it] still permits the violation of the freedom of occupation of migrant workers (and hence the denial of their economic agency); does not guarantee them the right to live with members of their family (and is thus liable to suspend their motherhood); does not recognize these restrictions as mechanisms that render them disadvantaged (thereby upholding the sharp distinction between migrant workers and victims); and gives migrant workers no access to citizenship. (Wagner, 2010: 76)[13]

Exclusion from equal citizenship and rights in Israel prompts migrants to create "inhabitable spaces of welcome" for themselves, as anthropologist Sarah Willen (2007) notes in explaining how migrant workers with and especially without visas can form spaces in which they feel a sense of belonging and of being protected and wanted in a host society that in itself is culturally split and divided. These spaces include all types of networks and organizations that contribute to the creation of an inclusive and enabling living space. The concept offers a way of understanding how migrant workers, legal or illegal, actively pursue ways that they can feel connected, stable, and secure in their fragile and labile existential context. From this perspective, small organizations are as beneficial as large ones. Spontaneous initiatives that meet the basic needs of existence, as much as organizations designed to promote the community, its culture, religion, and forms of recreation, are fruitful avenues for achieving greater stability and a sense of belonging (Sabar, 2008: 58–59). The urban metropolitan environment is the central sphere in which these processes of belonging take place.

BELONGING IN LIMINAL SITUATIONS

Patt Luluquisin is an artist who paints and takes photographs. After working in the software industry for several years, she turned to caregiving, arriving in Israel to work for an elderly woman. Her photograph *Sad* (2012) was taken at her current workplace, Ahuzat Poleg, a sheltered housing complex close to Kibbutz Tel Yitzhak (Figure 32). The photograph captures a moment in the life of one of the male residents in the institution, as Luluquisin explains.

> I'm intimately involved with all of the subjects I photograph. It's always important to me that I succeed in capturing the depths of the feelings of my subjects. I want to convey them to the viewer so that when they look at the photo, they feel what I felt when I took it. I think that that's a feeling of involvement, because I don't only take a photo for its beauty, but it also connects me to the feelings and situation that existed at the time. I took this photograph when they had a musical evening. I saw this man listening to the music, but to me it looked as though his thoughts were wandering far afield. He suddenly felt a great sadness because of something deep and distant that had happened to him, and I connected with that. (Luluquisin, interview by author, 2012)

Another photograph in that series is titled *Waiting* (Figure 33), of which Luluquisin says:

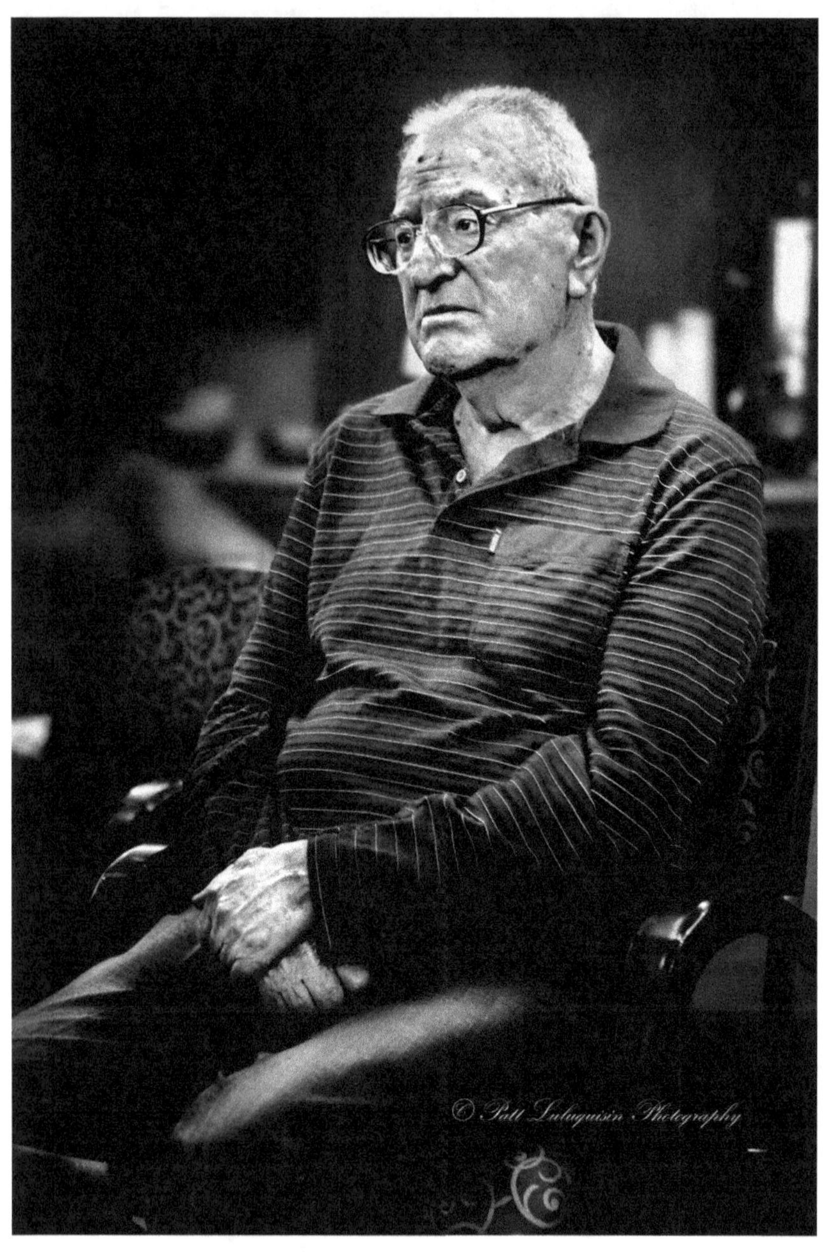

FIGURE 32. Patt Luluquisin, *Sad*, 2012. Black and white photo.

> The woman is sitting with her back to the camera, her feet crossed. At first glance, it looks like a nice, calm picture. The body posture appears to indicate to the viewer that the elderly woman is completely relaxed, as though comfortable—in that chair and in all other general aspects. But you can find another layer in the scene depicted in the photograph. The source of light serves as a hint. The light comes from the direction of the open door opposite the woman, as though declaring that she's sitting waiting for someone. Perhaps hoping someone will remember that she's there and come visit. . . . I identified with that pain she felt. . . . Perhaps I sound sentimental, but this is really in my personality. I don't take photos for fun. I want the viewer to become more involved and concerned about other people's feelings and experiences. In essence, this is the core of life. We're a society that is composed of different people. I want the viewers of my photos to see that many different things happen to different people in this world of ours. (Luluquisin, interview by author, 2012)

Luluquisin's photographs constitute a personal, loving, compassionate gaze that seeks to create a sense of community. Even though she is regarded as a foreigner and a temporary worker in this community, she is also a concrete and valuable part of it. Through her photographs she offers a critical gaze that enfolds within it a double perspective: a gaze from afar as an outsider and a close, intimate gaze as a caregiver who spends almost all her time with her employer and other elderly people, coming to know them in a way that even their biological families do not. It is a gaze that is simultaneously immediate and remote, one that demarcates the new borders of belonging and community in an age of transnationalism and migration of mass working forces around the world.

COMMUNITY

Female migrant workers' relations with the local community in Israel are varied and sometimes ambivalent. Some do not seek to be accepted in Israeli society and culture; many in fact choose to live in their homeland culture and prefer to be distinguished by their uniqueness as a separate community in Israel. A smaller number seek to assimilate as much as possible into Israeli society—by marrying an Israeli, for example. Most,

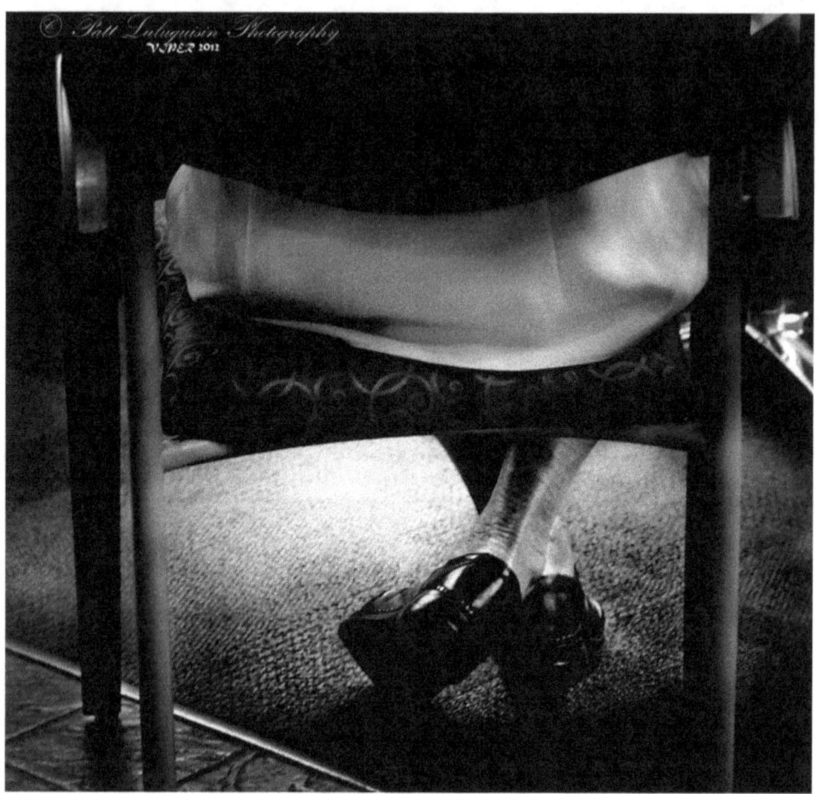

FIGURE 33. Patt Luluquisin, *Waiting*, 2012. Black and white photo.

however, choose to involve themselves with both countries and to identify with both cultures. Many of the artists among them photograph what they see as symbolizing their homeland and in-group, creating images of popular Filipino food, women in traditional costumes, religious ceremonies, and sacred Christian objects. At the same time, they also photograph the landscapes of Israel, documenting their visits to tourist sites with their friends and sending home pictures of celebration, such as Israel's Independence Day.

Ali Marasigan is a caregiver to an 80-year-old woman who lives in north Tel Aviv. Throughout her life she has had an inclination toward art, being engaged in creativity and arts even before coming to Israel. In Israel she plays an active and prominent part in the Filipino community's events. In preparation for a competition of costumes from different regions and

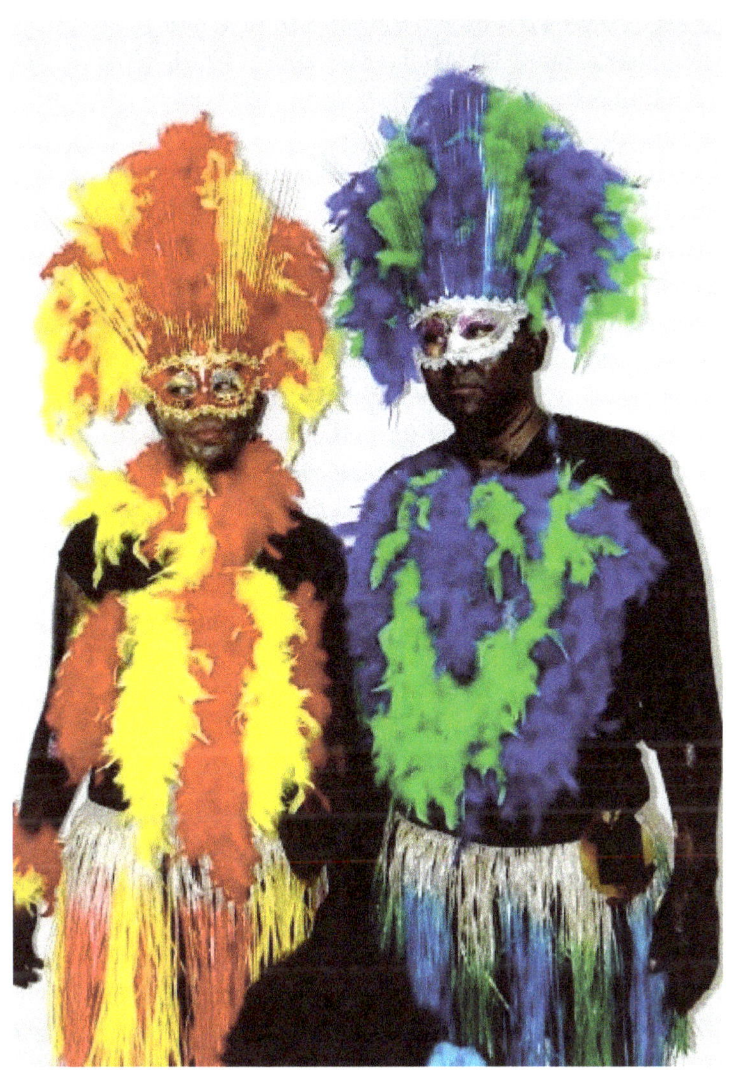

Figure 34. Ali Marasigan, Untitled, 2012. Color photo.

districts in the Philippines held in 2012, for example, she purchased all the necessary materials from a shop in south Tel Aviv and, with a team of friends, created a costume from her own region of the country, winning first place (Figure 34). Migrant workers in Israel, in particular those from the Philippines and African countries, relatively quickly fuse into a dense fabric of organizations and societies they create for themselves to meet basic human physical, emotional, and spiritual needs (Sabar, 2008: 18–19). The webs spun in these collective networks through their activities create communal patterns of life, a shared home, and an experience of stability and roots (29).

Most of the female migrant workers live in a dialectic experience, creating a pseudo-kinship system that operates in accordance with rules similar to those in real kinship networks, but their belonging is determined on the basis of other criteria. These systems form living communities and initiatives that are not based on blood and traditional family relations; the members serve as a support for each other (Sabar, 2008: 46).

The members of the Filipino community in Israel have a vibrant community life, centered in south Tel Aviv. The area around the central bus station teems with shops that cater to the community (e.g., Filipino goods, foods, and telephone and Internet services) and places of recreation around which the community's activity revolves. Further evidence of this life is found in the monthly English-Tagalog magazine *Manila Tel Aviv*, which provides entertainment articles, reports from the Philippine embassy in Israel, and news from the Philippines, Israel, and around the world. Distributed at the central Tel Aviv bus station and at other Filipino meeting places, its title attests to its transnational identity, which shifts between Manila, the capital of the Philippines, and Tel Aviv, the central place of residence and activity of the Filipino community in Israel.

Vibrant artistic activity is another characteristic of the Filipino community in Israel, such as the Filipino Clickers Association and the Pinoy Photographers Society in Israel. The Pinoy Photographers Society started as an independent organization of Filipino photographers working in Israel. These organizations do not receive any state funding and act completely independently. I met several of the members in one such organization and conducted in-depth interviews with four—Marylou Muga, Sharon Miguel, Patt Luluquisin, and Jenny Cajes.[14] For most of the artists in the organization, photography is a hobby; for a minority, a

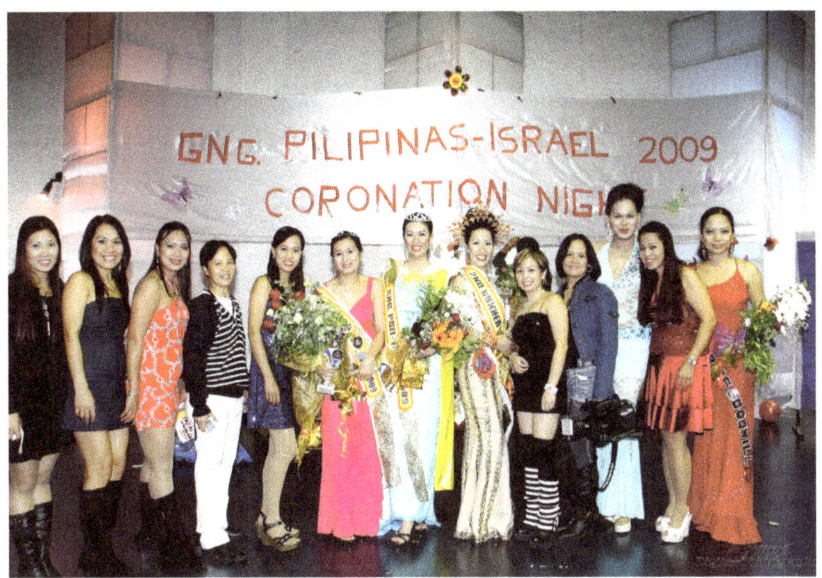

FIGURE 35. Jenny Cajes, Untitled, 2009. Color photo.

profession. Its members are responsible for enlisting new members, creating and running the website, holding study workshops and photography trips throughout the country, and organizing celebratory events. Within its artistic and social world its members can act as sovereign agents.

Jenny Cajes serves as one of the Filipino community's official photographers in Israel. From time to time she is invited to document community events organized independently by the community as well as organized events at the Philippine embassy. She also runs a private business for photographic projects in Ramat Gan, a city east of Tel Aviv. The photo in Figure 35 was taken during the crowning of the Filipina beauty queen, an annual event held in Tel Aviv. The photograph captures a less official moment, as the four winners are joined onstage by various women of the community—the organizers, family members, and friends—to be photographed together. All of them receive representation and commemoration through the act of photographing.

The background behind the group reveals a public structure of some kind, decorated with a simple textile banner in honor of the event. The decorations will be taken down and the space will resume its normal function right after the event is over. Although the location is a small community center and the decorations modest, the women have obviously invested substantial efforts in designing the event and decorating the hall, thereby actively constructing their identity as individuals and as a social group. As agents, they express their hybrid identity—an identity that refuses to be defined as one-dimensional but rather as proactive, conducting itself along a continuum of identities, shifting between Filipino culture and Israeli existence.

CONCLUSION

Female migrant workers cultivate a transnational identity based on their homeland culture and maintained by the ongoing relations—economic, political, religious, and other—with their country of origin. At the same time, however, their identity and lives are nourished by elements in the host country. Their artwork includes a reflexive gaze on their intrarelations with the Filipino community residing in Israel as much as on their complex relations with veteran Israelis—mutual relations that influence both sides and change them in ways that are not always easy to define.

Listening to the experiences of female migrant workers in Israel reveals new questions that highlight the need for contemporary conceptualization of their multilayered and relative status, both in Israeli society and in their country of origin. Among the questions that arise, it is especially interesting to ask whether they are sovereign agents who make use of resourceful ways to build their lives and future, constructing new channels of income and accumulating knowledge by freely deciding to move to another country, or whether migration is an act imposed on them as a result of circumstances, including the accelerated development of globalization in the country of origin and in the host country (Piper, 2008). The answer to this question is neither simple nor straightforward. Although they are clearly excluded from agency in the liberal discourse, as Roy Wagner and others recognize, the stories of their lives nonetheless evince changing and diverse levels of agency.

Following the growing body of knowledge about this subject, I suggest that a deeper and more complex understanding of the ways in which female migrant workers perceive their experiences should be sought. One of the key ways in which this can be accomplished is by listening to their stories and acknowledging their knowledge of their situation and lives. The artworks discussed here are one such way. The thought-provoking pieces of art created by Filipina women reveal the internal dialogue they conduct with themselves as well as their reading and understanding of the various kinds of relations they maintain while living in the Israeli space. These include not only their immediate environment, the members of the Filipino community, and family and friends in their homeland but also Israeli citizens. Here, too, they demonstrate the way their position forms part of a complex, stratified process of continuous identity formation—a fluid and labile identity that refuses to be reduced to just one element. Some are committed to preserving their original traditions and minimizing their contact with the host society. Others adopt as many features of Israeli culture as they can. Most, however, combine a mix of attitudes and manage to create a balance between the two extremes.

Filipina migrant workers do not constitute a monolithic group but are diverse subjects who express varied levels of agency derived from an array of parameters—education, class, degree of religiosity, family status, personality traits, and so on. Migrant workers can come from rural areas or major metropolises. They can be highly accomplished and educated or have only a basic education. All these variables and parameters join the reality they encounter upon their arrival in Israel. Examples abound. In most cases, female migrant workers find themselves in an inferior position to their employer, who is an Israeli citizen in terms of monetary freedom and freedom to move in public spaces. They do not speak the local language and are unfamiliar with local conduct. They are Christians in a country with a Jewish majority. They are at high risk of having their rights violated and are often cut off from their homes and families. On other occasions, they find work that allows them to develop and accumulate various kinds of new knowledge, skills, and money. Some of the women choose to change their status and receive Israeli citizenship, by marrying an Israeli (Hacker, 2009). Others return home with the money and knowledge they have gained and are esteemed by their families for having provided for them so long.

One striking feature is nonetheless common to all Filipina migrant workers in Israel: the feeling of dialectically shifting between great proximity (caring daily for elderly and disabled people and befriending them) and extreme foreignness and alienation (being the ultimate Other in society and in official law). A striking example of these perplexing feelings can be found in Angie Hsu's dissertation, "You Have Your Own Country: Filipina Migrants 'Beyond Citizenship' in the Jewish State," which was submitted to the Gender Institute at the London School of Economics in 2011. Hsu, a resident of Hong Kong who lived in Israel and volunteered at the Kav LaOved organization, describes this positioning by quoting a Filipina living in Israel: "Sometimes I feel that I am already a member here, because they treat me like their own. . . . Sometimes, though, I also feel—when I get news about my children, news that they're going to send them back to the Philippines, to their own country—I feel like I'm not still part of this country" (Hsu, 2011: 34).

4

Conclusion

The life experiences and insights of migrant women that were introduced in this volume function as a window onto a contemporary social moment. The extensive scholarly literature on migration published over the past two decades illustrates how, by preserving links and relationships with people and organizations from their countries of origin and by developing new links in their new countries of residence, individuals and groups who migrate exist not within the borders of any single nation-state but rather in a transnational space. The mobility of goods, currencies, and people around the globe is greater than ever before, and with the growing reach of mass media and Internet communication, careers, family lives, and monetary activities stretch across the globe. These profound changes in transnational activity produce a complex set of interactions and relations that coexist simultaneously across various nation-states.

The women surveyed in this volume, despite their many differences, are linked by a unified fundamental logic: Each one of them has been deeply affected by the international context and political-economic interests that have prompted waves of migration around the globe. Thus the immigration to Israel of Ethiopian and FSU Jews was a direct consequence of the domino effect of the collapse of the communist regime in the Soviet Union, and the arrival of Filipina migrant workers in Israel is related to developments in the Israeli-Palestinian conflict on the one hand and to global economic trends that marked the beginning of the transnational age on the other. The unique circumstances of the Israeli case notwithstanding, migrant women in Israel who arrived from various countries since the mid-1980s share many experiences and take part in the contemporary worldwide phenomenon of mass migration. These global and local movements constitute a rich field of inquiry into the complex dynamics of the political, economic, and cultural power relations between states and their citizens and between different groups and individuals within a single nation-state (Yuval-Davis et al., 2005: 522).

The present historical moment is particularly suited to an exploration of the subject of migration within the framework of transnationalism. The event that marks the symbolic launching of the era known as transnationalism is, as noted earlier, the 1989 fall of the Berlin Wall, followed by the collapse of the Eastern bloc, which contributed to the acceleration of economic and cultural globalization and prompted theorists to herald the breaking down of boundaries and the "end of history" (Fukuyama, 1989). But the terror attacks of September 11, 2001, marked a new turning point, severely dampening the illusion of a borderless global village and the attendant attempts to universalize the world by imposing Western economic and cultural paradigms. Perceived in the West as a terror attack on a global scale, the events of 9/11 reinforced the sense that nation-states had to bolster rather than dismantle their borders and tighten controls on immigration, which was now feared and seen as a growing threat. In Western thought the idea of the end of history began losing ground in favor of national borders, a direction articulated as early as 1993 by Samuel Huntington in *The Clash of Civilizations and the Remaking of World Order*. Huntington argued that "states are the primary, indeed, the only important actors in world affairs" (Huntington, 1997: 33). Today, this vision is far less controversial than it was when his book first appeared.

From the present vantage point, more than a decade after 9/11 and more than two decades after the fall of the Berlin Wall, we can observe that the phenomenon defined in the early 1990s as globalization now manifests itself more precisely as transnationalism. The renunciation of nation-states and the eradication of borders are now broadly understood as a momentary vision that has vanished, perhaps irretrievably, and the transnational discourse is currently the most useful approach for making sense of global power relations and dynamics in general and of the global phenomenon of mass migration in particular.

Although nation-states are of seminal importance and largely responsible for shaping the experience of migrants, the logic of transnationalism suggests that the movement of mass groups of migrants also challenges the notion of the nation-state and undermines the premise that national identity parallels national territory, a notion exemplified in attitudes toward citizenship and national identity. According to this logic, migrants find themselves as living simultaneously in their old and new home states. Whereas the government and institutions of the recipient nation-state typically seek to regulate the lives of migrants, the migrants themselves are not passive objects controlled by the state but rather active subjects who participate in molding their own fate; they engage in creative agency, such as intercommunity praxis, and propose political and ethical alternatives to state policies.

The attempt to trace or define with precision those state actions that govern the lives of migrants is always precarious, but this is doubly true of Israel, in particular with regard to the policies that apply to migrant women. Lacking a stable and comprehensive migration policy, especially one that applies to non-Jewish migrants but also to various degrees to Jewish migrants, the state and its various representatives manifest a wide range of stances toward migrants rather than a unified position.[1] The many players in the field, including the state, civic institutions, and residents of the country, are influenced by fluctuating attitudes and interests, resulting in frequent changes of policy; inconsistencies in policy interpretation and implementation affect the lives of migrants in diverse and complicated ways. This unstable reality leads to countless manifestations of discrimination and exclusion. For example, Ethiopian immigrants face challenges on many different fronts, including segregated classes in schools and discriminatory health policies. The Jewish identity of many of the FSU immigrants is questioned by the Orthodox rabbinate, which demands that they convert and imposes on them marriage and burial restrictions. Migrant workers employed as caregivers have to contend with constantly changing policies and restrictions laid down by different officials with divergent and frequently conflicting interests. The most extreme example of this fluctuation is the Interior Ministry regulation, later tempered by Israel's Supreme Court, to deport female migrant workers who give birth while in Israel.

Even though the transnational age has brought the role of the nation-state to the fore once again, the question of the nation-state's competence and governmentality is complex and much less well understood than commonly assumed. The view that a more or less fixed, binary relationship exists between the recipient society and migrants in the nation-state must similarly be revised in light of the recognition that the interaction between these social groups is highly labile. As Julia Lerner notes in her study of FSU immigrant culture, "[It is] not a culture in dialogue with Israeli culture or a culture that influences Israeli culture but a culture fabricated within Israel, in the midst and out of Israeliness" (Lerner, 2012: 23). This complex reality gives birth to new insights into the question of belonging (or "absorption," in Israeli-Jewish terms) and affords a fresh view of migrants, veterans, and the relationship between them.

As I have argued throughout the book, in the age of transnationalism no simple lines demarcate incoming groups as closer to or farther removed from the Israeli state and veteran society in terms of religion, race, or any other dimension, not even in the supposedly obvious distinction between Jews and non-Jews. The prevalent claim that migrant or intergroup integration is dependent on reducing differences and increasing society's homogeneity in line with the hegemonic majority has been shown by others to be specious (Lerner, 2012: 30).

Immigration changes not only the immigrants but also the recipient society. Veteran citizens cannot be regarded as a fixed group with static features facing a clearly distinguishable migrant population passing through various stages of assimilation or segregation. This binary organizational principle must be replaced with a more complex reading of reality as a field in which all subjects, veterans and migrants alike, necessarily undergo a dynamic reconstruction of their identity and an ongoing re-repositioning of themselves in relation to others. In this respect, the analysis of migrant groups is also an analysis of the recipient society, revealing a great deal about its structure and the challenges it faces. In particular, I have argued that the society as a whole is immersed in ongoing power relations, with each group fighting for symbolic and concrete power. As the newcomers try to pave their way in the dense field of power relations of the host country, the hegemony strives to maintain its own power and characteristics and therefore repeatedly rearticulates its essence and boundaries in conjunction with the immigrants' redefinitions. These processes, aimed at maintaining the hegemony's superiority, often produce racist and sexist manifestations toward various immigrant groups.

In the context of migration studies, Israel must be recognized as a unique democratic society because of its ethnonational definition as the Jewish homeland. This yields a unique blend of transnational migration and Jewish immigration, the two types differing in their nature, goals, and reception in Israel. Jewish immigrants often identify closely with Israel, their new old homeland, and although some regard the ethos of "returning to Zion" as antiquated and irrelevant in a post-Zionist age, many Jewish citizens of Israel still think that ancient and modern Jewish history, in particular the Holocaust, makes the State of Israel more than just their territorial home. Their sense of belonging is therefore unlike that experienced, for example, by Mexican immigrants in the United States or Russians in Germany. The emotions and ideology inherent in Jewish immigration to Israel render the country's social landscape unique in the transnational world.

The distinctive phenomenon of Jewish immigration to Israel (aliyah) serves to highlight facets of the other types of migration to the country, primarily economic migration of non-Jews, as in the case of the Filipina migrant workers explored in this study. The fact that these women are marginalized on four counts—class, nationality, religion, and gender—underscores Israel's status as an ethnonational state and the correspondingly deeper exclusion experienced by these migrants (Yuval-Davis et al., 2005: 526–27). Established by and for Jewish immigrants, Israel offers non-Jewish migrants only limited possibilities of becoming citizens or fully integrating into its society. Ironically, however, it is the migrant Filipinas, living on the margins of Israeli society, who arguably mount the greatest challenge to the absolutist, binary definitions of proximity and distance, belonging and alienation. Employed primarily as caregivers, these migrants come into constant and intimate contact with Israelis, living in their homes and taking care of their elderly parents, their children, and their disabled members.

Thus contemporary Israel possesses a dynamic community of different kinds of subjects, some veteran migrants and some relatively new, characterized by a complex set of relationships. Julia Kristeva wrote about the notion of the stranger, the foreigner, the outsider, who resides in a country or a nation and about the notion of strangeness within the self throughout Western history and up to the contemporary era: "[A] paradoxical community is emerging . . . made up of foreigners who are reconciled with themselves to the extent that they recognize themselves as foreigners" (Kristeva, 1991: 195).

This community of foreigners shapes the lives of the migrant women discussed in this volume and forms the basis for their hybrid, mutable identities. As I have argued, in the Israeli case, as in other nation-states around the world, we cannot speak of a single identity of the migrant subject but must recognize the presence of a complex set of intersecting categories of identity perpetually interacting with and affecting one another. This notion is informed by such feminist scholars as Inderpal Grewal (Grewal, 2005; Kaplan and Grewal, 1999), Chakravorty Gayatri Spivak (Spivak, 1988), and Chandra Talpade Mohanty (Mohanty, 2003), who were among the founding mothers of transnational feminist cultural studies. They insist on an intersectional analysis that offers solidarity which is not based on an oppressive, colonizing power but rather offers perspectives that cut across social groups and borders. With respect to the identity-construction processes of migrant women in their new country, the boundaries and strata of identity—whether real, imagined, unified, or hyphenated—are multifaceted, manifesting themselves in the lives and consciousness of migrants by numerous means. Migration involves the active and long-term administration of an economy of identities, among them gender identity, which relates to both the country left behind and the new country of residence.

The artworks of the migrant women featured in this book function as anchors for a fuller understanding of the women's overlapping narratives and their bearing on the individual and collective experience of migrant women in Israel. The themes addressed in their art yield information and knowledge, both verbal and nonverbal, that are different in nature from sources drawn from statistical demographic reports and similar data. Their art speaks volubly of their experiences as migrants, articulating subversive statements and challenging the norms and myths of the supposedly stable and monolithic identity and hegemonic characteristics (national, ethnic, religious, gendered, etc.) of the society in which they live.

The course of life of a migrant woman cannot be reduced to a simple linear path that begins with the migrant leaving her home to go to a new country, in which the veteran society or state laws exercise their power over her, and ends with the migrant overcoming challenges and becoming an autonomous subject whose full potential is realized in the recipient society. Migrant women live in a complex, multifaceted reality that is at once progressive and conservative, empowering and weakening, liberating and binding. They are affected by external factors, including the central fact that they live in a patriarchal society that discriminates against women in fields such as religion, but they are also forced to resist and act against economic and political oppression (in both their homeland and their adopted country) and to find resourceful ways of handling oppressive constitutional laws and various social policies and praxis.

Negotiating this complex matrix as part of the process of constructing their identities requires sophisticated skills on the part of migrant women. The factors that shape identity span a broad spectrum that includes issues of race, class, and gender. Thus migrants in Israel cope with many class-related challenges involving, for example, education and income; with race-related challenges, such as stereotyping and cultural differences; with marital and other personal status restrictions resulting from their contested religious status; and with gender-related challenges, including sexual violence and laws that affect the migrant women's rights with respect to fertility, pregnancy, and motherhood. Class and race are identity categories that intersect with gender in various ways, frequently as a factor that compounds discrimination, as, for example, in the case of the systematic discrimination against women in the work market or the racist attitude toward women of color that accompanies sexist stereotyping. The 1.5 generation also encounters the additional gender-related challenge of arriving in a new country during the sensitive period of transition from girlhood to womanhood, thus facing the need to construct a new personal, gendered, and national identity all at the same time.

But these women do not just encounter challenges and experience setbacks or feel crushed under oppressive forces. They always maintain a strong sense of subjectivity and developed agency, which they practice in various resourceful ways. Examples include Philippine women who take courses in different fields of knowledge, offered by local community centers, in topics such as economics and politics, English and Hebrew language skills, photography and computer design, and thus do not restrict their activity to only caregiving. When they graduate from these courses, they sometimes even volunteer to become instructors to other Philippine women or travel back to their country of origin with knowledge that is much appreciated by the local people in the Philippines. Women who emigrated from Ethiopia can and indeed do make use of affirmative action laws and regulations to enter higher education institutions with full scholarships and then make their way to influential positions in the public sector, as more than a few women actually did (several became lawyers; one is currently a member of the Tel Aviv Municipality; another was a member of parliament). Women who emigrated from the former Soviet Union also find resourceful ways to develop and gain agency by using the great mass of other FSU women and men living in Israel to initiate commercial enterprises, to be elected to political positions, and to mainstream Russian culture into Israeli society, thus turning from objects to subjects of culture.

A gender analysis of migration helps to deepen our understanding of the political nature of migration in a transnational world. Several studies show that gender plays a different and crucial part in the conduct of men and women who migrate. In her study from 2012 sociologist Lilach Lev Ari found that migrant men maintain a lesser degree of transnational connections than migrant women, who tend to maintain a more intense degree of transnational activity (Lev Ari, 2012: 229). Moreover, as scholar Nira Yuval-Davis remarks, women are often constructed as symbolic border guards of ethnic and national collectivities and therefore studying them carefully can carry valuable understandings about the complex interrelations between nation-states, women, and culture (Yuval-Davis, 1997). Gender, the only identity category common to all the migrant artists discussed in this volume, is revealed as a highly political category. Moreover, the documentation and analysis of processes of identity formation among migrant women is an act that constructs a feminist body of knowledge that seeks to free itself from patriarchal logic. Turning to the sources of knowledge themselves—that is, to the women—averts the problem of speaking in their name and promotes a clearer understanding of migrant women's lives in the global sense; at the same time, it offers fresh understandings about the particular case of migrant women in the Israeli ethnonational context.

Notes

INTRODUCTION

1. Contemporary feminist research insists on questioning two of the significant foci of knowledge determined in the wake of the crisis of representation: the voice and the experience. This stance advocates that the subject is not an authentic representation of the self but a discursive product shaped by an encounter with various ideological discourse regimes. Because voice and experience are discursive products—the voice is not simply "there," and experiences do not merely "happen" to women—I acknowledge that we cannot be satisfied with just "making a voice heard" as a political project for its own sake.
2. The Law of Return aims to enable the immigration of all Jews to Israel. Under this law, immigrants are eligible for an unusually quick naturalization process, which grants them full citizenship immediately upon arrival. The Law of Return has symbolic and practical aspects insofar as it both symbolizes and realizes the status of Israel as the state of the Jews. For more, see Ernst (2009) and Perez (2011).
3. Important scholarship on immigrant women from Arab lands living in Israel has been published over the years, and although this literature refers to a different time frame than in this current volume (one not affected by the collapse of the Soviet bloc or within the framework of the 1.5 generation of women in a transnational age), it is important to mention the contribution of Mizrahi scholars such as Dahan-Kalev (2014), Nagar-Ron and Motzafi-Haller (2011), and Shohat (2006).
4. Intersectional analysis allows us to introduce multiple identity categories to further understand the particularities of every subject's position (parameters such as living in the center or periphery of the country, level of education, physical abilities, sexual orientation, and age). Because of the scope of this book, I was unable to include additional categories that could have explained in more detail the stratification points of each artist discussed and

her artistic decisions. Moreover, two of the artists included in this project are closeted lesbians and were willing to participate only on the condition that I do not discuss that aspect of their lives.

5. See Antebi-Yemini (2010), Arian et al. (2009), Ben-Ezer (2010), Kemp and Raijman (2008), Lerner and Feldhay (2012), Lomsky-Feder and Rapoport (2010), Sabar (2008), Sikron and Leshem (1998), Wagner (2010: 61–90), and Wurgaft (2006).
6. The interviews were conducted in Hebrew by me, if not indicated otherwise, and the translations are mine.
7. In this stance I follow important statements of previous feminist projects in the arts, such as the one articulated by art historians Maura Reilly and Linda Nochlin in their 2007 mega exhibition *Global Feminisms: New Directions in Contemporary Art*: "We did not expect women from Bolivia or Pakistan to exhibit specific ethnic traits in their art, any more than we expected the same from an artists from the U.S.; to do so would have been naïve and patronizing. Yet we were open to, and very interested in, the varying and innovative ways that women from diverse parts of the world self-consciously deployed the visual culture they had inherited to create new, often critical visual expression" (Reilly and Nochlin, 2007: 11).

CHAPTER 1

1. Tamara is a common Israeli name, and Natasha is a typically Russian name.
2. For more about migration during adolescence, see Horowitz (1998).
3. Despite a state medal awarded to all mothers of five to ten children, the average number of children per woman was one (Kiblitskaya, 2000).
4. Research shows that Jewish FSU migrant women who move to other countries than Israel, such as the United States, do not suffer from the same stigmatization (Remennick, 2007: 245–78).
5. The subject of prostitution is complex, and feminist attitudes toward it cover a wide range, from the urgent call to stamp it out in all its forms to acceptance of women's active agency when prostitution forms a means of escape from violent situations, exploitation, or extreme economic hardship (Kempadoo et al., 2005).
6. See www.birthrightisrael.com/Pages/Default.aspx (accessed March 12, 2016).
7. See www.jafi.org.il/NR/rdonlyres/5D5280AA-A513-4BEA-A068-08676F872943/0/Selahsc.pdf (accessed March 12, 2016).

8. This prayer, in the masculine form, is recited every morning by observant Jews.
9. In the Israeli cultural imagination, all FSU migrants are identified with right-wing politics. Thus, for example, historian Dimitri Chomsky describes the link between right-wing Israeli politics and the Russian essence in this way: "The legislative anti-democratic tendencies could not stand up to such as these without decisive support from Soviet anti-democratic tendencies. . . . Many of the FSU immigrants and the majority of their representatives in the Knesset [Israeli parliament] not only find it difficult to free themselves of the conceptual baggage of the Soviet dictatorship but even proudly embrace it" (cited in Galili and Bronfman, 2013: 14). Other scholars point out that antidemocratic and oppressive attitudes toward various groups, even before the arrival of FSU migrants, have been present in Israel since the state's establishment and that they therefore predate the Soviet immigration and beckoned and appealed to it rather than relied on its support (Reider, 2013). In actuality, many FSU migrants identify with center and even left-wing politics.
10. The Hebrew word for "refugee" is *palit*. The exhibition's title in Hebrew is thus "cosmo-palit," a play on "cosmopolitan."
11. My thanks go to Dr. Tal Ben Zvi for allowing me to use the fruit of her research regarding Masha Rubin.
12. See www.haokets.org/2013/04/27 (accessed May 26, 2013).

CHAPTER 2

1. Several American Jewish organizations, including the NACOE (North American Conference on Ethiopian Jewry), the AAEJ (American Association for Ethiopian Jews), and the JDC (Joint Distribution Committee), assisted in raising awareness among the American and Israeli governments about the need to help Ethiopian Jewry realize their decision to emigrate (Kraft, 2013).
2. All public buildings in Israel post a guard at the entrance to check the bags of everyone entering as a precaution to prevent terror attacks.
3. For the status of women in Africa in general, see Sabar (2010).
4. Despite the difference between Ethiopia and Israel, however, it should be remembered that patriarchal norms do not exist only in Ethiopia but Israeli society itself also remains patriarchal, although taking different, more elusive forms.

5. The discriminatory tendency in the Israeli education system continues to today, finding expression in particular in the policy of forcing Ethiopian children into the special needs framework. Petitions and reports from various organizations indicate that since 2005 almost double the number of Ethiopian students have been placed in this educational system than non-Ethiopian students (Nesher, 2012).
6. It should be stressed that black African Jews are considered a rare phenomenon, because throughout (Western) history, Jews were thought to originate from Europe or Arab countries only. As mentioned earlier, black Jews in Israel today make up less than 2% of the population, or about 135,000 people.
7. My thanks go to Dr. Dalia Markovitch for sharing her thoughts with me regarding Esti Almo-Wexler's works.
8. See the critical article, posted by academic and social activists Hananya Vanda and Adana Zawdu on the Young Ethiopian Students (YES) blog on July 3, 2010, depicting the way in which a vast scholarly industry has developed around Ethiopian migrants in Israel: "Al ha-kalkala ha-politit shel 'mada'ei ha-yahadut etiopoa' ve-al trumatam shel yehuday etiopia le-kalkala u-le-chevra ha-yisraelit" [The Political Economy of "Ethiopian Jewish Studies" and the Contribution of Ethiopian Jews to Israeli Economy and Society], youngethiopianstudents.wordpress.com/2010/07/03 (accessed March 12, 2016) (Hebrew).
9. Many Ethiopian migrant women, especially those who arrived in Israel as adults, create artworks in forms that are regarded as traditional. Such works can be seen, for example, in the "Gedgeda" exhibition held at the Sadna Art Gallery (Rishon Lezion) in 2008 or in the items sold at the fair trade shop run by the Achoti movement in Tel Aviv. This kind of art possesses complex formal, thematic, and political aspects that deserve a separate study.
10. For a discussion of Jewish feminist art and Jewish ideas relating to female menstruation, see Sperber (2012).
11. "Mi yakhol/lo yakhol litrom dam" [Who Can/Can't Give Blood], Magen David Adom in Israel, www.mdais.org (accessed May 12, 2013) (Hebrew).
12. The Sigd is a special holiday of Ethiopian Jewry, symbolizing the acceptance of the Torah. Before emigrating from Ethiopia, the Beta Israel community would gather and pray on that day; since their arrival in Israel, it has become a special day of celebration in Jerusalem. In 2008 the Sigd was officially declared a national day in the State of Israel.
13. Demle's *Half Foreigners* is the fruit of an intense Internet correspondence over two years. The author shared his opinions and views on the contempo-

rary state of the Ethiopian community in Israel with visitors to his Facebook page, most of whom are part of that community. The volume refrains from adducing external voices and focuses on giving a platform to those within the community, covering a variety of stances that frequently oppose or contradict one another. Demle well describes the liminal position and feeling of hybridity that Ethiopian Jews experience: "On the one hand, we made every effort to immigrate to the Land and to become an integral part of it, and we're still paying our dues to society, like everyone else. On the other, that same society does not regard us as part of it. Every day we are told this loudly and clearly in various ways. Even those of us who are sure that we belong here come out confused. If a person doesn't have a stable identity and everything is precarious for him, he can't develop properly in a society of people and his sense of self-confidence will inevitably be harmed. So we can say that we are a small, different community living in Israeli society, very confused. We belong and we don't belong. We're present and absent at the same time. Half foreigners" (Demle, 2011: 66).

CHAPTER 3

1. For the correlation between global sex trafficking, women, and migrant workers, see Levenkron and Dahan (2003).
2. Rami Ben-David, Ministry of Interior, personal correspondence, April 25, 2013.
3. Most exhibitions devoted to the subject of migrant workers or refugees in Israel that have gained significant exposure in the public space have been held by Israeli artists and not by the migrant community itself.
4. The OECD has thirty-four members; Israel joined in 2010.
5. Protocol 69 of a meeting held on November 9, 2012, at the Israeli Knesset, to discuss the topic "Foreigners in Israel: The Findings of the Knesset Study." www.knesset.gov.il/protocols/data/rtf/zarim/2012-01-09.rtf (accessed March 13, 2016).
6. See www.tel-aviv.gov.il/Residents/HealthAndSocial/Pages/Mesila.aspx (accessed March 12, 2016).
7. See www.bostonmayday.org/chelsea_resolution.html (accessed March 12, 2016).
8. Rami Ben David, Ministry of Interior, personal correspondence, April 25, 2013.
9. Only Indian, Chinese, and Mexican migrants sent more money home that year. That could be explained by the fact that India and China are the larg-

est countries in the world, and the porous border between Mexico and the United States constitutes a major migration factor.

10. According to the National Statistical Coordination Board; see www.nscb.gov.ph/secstat/d_popn.asp (accessed March 13, 2016).
11. According to IBON data; ibon.org/2009/12/on-human-rights-day-25-million-filipinos-denied-right-to-work/ (accessed March 13, 2016). The IBON Foundation is an NGO for the active development of Filipinos; it was established in 1978, and its goal is to deal with social, economic, and political issues.
12. A "procedure" has a different status and implications than an official "rule." A procedure is an internal paper that gives clerks the authority to interpret and act as they see fit. A rule is unambiguous and all-encompassing. The fact that the status of pregnant migrant workers is dealt with as a procedure and not as a state rule reflects the sensitivity of the subject in the eyes of governmental institutions. By refusing to pass an official law, they are able to maintain a nonofficial discriminatory praxis on the ground.
13. The text of the International Convention on the Protection of the Rights of All Migrant Workers and Members of Their Families can be found at www.un.org/documents/ga/res/45/a45r158.htm (accessed March 12, 2016).
14. While writing this book, an exhibition titled *Inside and Outside the Picture: Filipino Migrant Workers Photograph in Israel*, was held in Tel Aviv and was devoted to photographs taken by members of the Pinoy Photographers Society in Israel (PPSI). The first of its kind in Israel, the exhibit was hosted by the Achoti Gallery in southern Tel Aviv in December 2012 and was curated by Shula Keshet, Vered Nissim, and Tal Dekel. The catalog is available on the Achoti website: www.achoti.org.il/?p=1542 (accessed March 8, 2016).

CHAPTER 4

1. Recall that in the Israeli context the term *migrant* designates an entirely different status than *immigrant*, which is reserved only for Jews (see Introduction).

Bibliography

Abate, Y. 1991. “The Role of Women.” In *A Country Study: Ethiopia*, ed. T. Ofcansky and B. LaVerle. Washington, DC: Federal Research Division, Library of Congress. lcweb2.loc.gov/cgi-bin/query/r?frd/cstdy:@field(DOCID+et0070) (accessed January 28, 2014).

Adar-Bechar, O. 2009. *Shti ve-erev: Ta'arukha bogrot* [Warp and Woof: Graduates' Exhibition]. Jerusalem: Emuna College (Hebrew).

Adega, A. 2000. *Mase el he-chalom* [Journey to the Dream]. Self-published (Hebrew).

Alcoff, L. M., and Mendieta, E., eds. 2007. *Identities: Race, Class, Gender, and Nationality*. Oxford: Wiley-Blackwell.

Almog, O., and Evdosin, I. 2013. “Me'afyanim ve-ve-hashpa'ot ha-aliyah mi-brit ha-mo'etzot” [The Features and Influence of the FSU Immigration]. www.peopleil.org/details.aspx?itemID=7571 (accessed March 2, 2016) (Hebrew).

Alon, K. 2013. “Ha-qol ha-nashi ha-mizrahi be-omanut ha-yisraelit: hetekh rochav” [The Feminine Mizrahi Voice in Israeli Art: A Broad Cross-Section]. In *Breaking Walls: Contemporary Mizrahi Feminist Artists*, ed. K. Alon and S. Keshet, 109–44. Tel Aviv: Achoti (Hebrew).

Ankori, G. 1993. “The Immigrant's Daughter: Frida Kahlo's ‘Other’ Identity.” *Proceedings of the World Congress of Jewish Studies* 2: 93–100.

Antebi-Yemini, L. 2005. “Tohara Bema'avar” [Purity in Transition]. In *Mulualem: Ethiopian Women and Girls in Spaces, Worlds, and Journeys Between Cultures*, ed. M. Shabtay and L. Kacen, 44–56. Tel Aviv: Lashon Tzaha (Hebrew).

———. 2010. “Be-shulay ha-nirut: olim etiopi'im be-yisrael” [On the Edge of Visibility: Ethiopian Immigrants in Israel]. In *Visibility in Immigration: Body, Gaze, Representation*, ed. E. Lumsky-Feder and T. Rapoport, 43–68. Jerusalem: Van Leer Institute (Hebrew).

Arian, A., Philippov, M., and Knafelman, A. 2009. *Auditing Israeli Democracy: Twenty Years of Immigration from the Soviet Union*. Israeli Democracy Index 2009. Jerusalem: Israel Democracy Institute (Hebrew).

Armon Azoulay, E. 2012. "Biqur studio: zey lo le-shidur" [Studio Visit: Not For Broadcasting]. *Haaretz* (*Galleriya*), May 4: 5 (Hebrew).

Ashwin, S. 2002. "'A Woman Is Everything': The Reproduction of Soviet Ideals of Womanhood in Post-Communist Russia." In *Work, Employment, and Transition: Reconstructing Livelihood in Post-Communist Russia*, ed. A. Smith, A. Rainnie, and A. Swain, 117–33. London: Routledge.

Balibar, E. 1988. "Is There a Neo-Racism?" In *Race, Nation, Class: Ambiguous Identities*, ed. E. Balibar and I. Wallerstein, 17–28. Paris: Editions la Découverte.

Basok, M., and Zarchia, T. 2010. "Ha-yo'etz shel ha-otzar: Ha-olim me-chever ha-medinot ba'u beglal ha-kesef" [The Treasury's Adviser: FSU Immigrants Have Come Because of the Money]. *Haaretz*, December 27 (Hebrew). www.haaretz.co.il/news/education/1.1237227 (accessed February 27, 2016).

Beauvoir, S. de. 2010 [1949]. *The Second Sex*. New York: Vintage.

Bekya, D., Tigeb, T., Tesema, Y., Massassa, O., Ondemagan, E., Mekonon, N., Qasya, M., and Prada-Gozu, S. 2013. *Sipur masa: Ha-aliya me-etiopia derekh sudan* [Story of a Journey: Immigration from Ethiopia via Sudan]. Haifa: Pardes (Hebrew).

Ben-Eliezer, U. 2008. "Kushi Sambo, bili bili bambo: Kaytzad yehudi hofekh shachor be-eretz ha-muvtachat" [Nigger Sambo, Billy Billy Bambo: How a Jew Becomes Black in the Promised Land]. In *Racism in Israel*, ed. Y. Shenhav and Y. Yona, 130–57. Jerusalem: Van Leer Institute, and Tel Aviv: Hakibbutz Hameuchad (Hebrew).

Ben-Ezer, G. 2010. "Ke-tipa el ha-yam? Nirut ve-I nirut shel yehudi etiopia be-hevra ha-yisraelit" [Like a Drop in the Ocean? The Visibility and Invisibility of Ethiopian Immigrants in Israel]. In *Visibility in Immigration: Body, Gaze, Representation*, ed. E. Lumsky-Feder and T. Rapoport, 305–28. Jerusalem: Van Leer Institute (Hebrew).

Benjamin, O. 2011. "Gender Outcomes of Labor Market Policy in Israel." *Equality, Diversity, and Inclusion: An International Journal* 30.5: 394–408.

Benjamin, O., Bernstein, D., and Motzafi-Haller, P. 2010. "Emotional Politics in Cleaning Work: The Case of Israel." *Human Relations* 64.3: 337–59.

Ben-Raphael, E. 2001. "Collective Identity in Israel." In *Reflection of a Society: In Memory of Yonathan Shapiro*, ed. H. Herzog, 489–514. Tel Aviv: Ramot (Hebrew).

Benton, M., and Garbuz, Y. 2009. *Anna Yam: Comfortable Anxiety*. Exhibition catalog. Tel Aviv: Braverman Gallery (Hebrew).

Ben Zvi, T. 2001. "Deferring Language as a Theme in the Work of Mizrahi Artists." In *Eastern Appearance/Mother Tongue: A Present That Stirs in the Thickets of Its Arab Past*, ed. Y. Nizri, 154–84. Tel Aviv: Babel.

———. 2011. *3 For 10*. Exhibition catalog. Holon: Israeli Center for Digital Art.

Bonacich, E., Alimohomed, S., and Wilson, J. 2008. "The Racialization of Global Labor." *American Behavioral Scientist* 52: 342–55.

Brookdale Institute. 2001. *Integration of Immigrants from Ethiopia in Israeli Society: Challenges, Policy, and Future Programs*. Jerusalem: JDC (Joint Distribution Committee) (Hebrew).

Broude, N. 1994. "The Pattern and Decoration Movement." In *The Power of Feminist Art*, ed. N. Broude and M. Garrard, 208–25. New York: Harry Abrams.

Buchsbaum, Y., Dagan, M., Diab, U., and Abramovitch, D. 2008. *Women Workers in a Precarious Employment Market*. Haifa: Mahut Center.

Butler, J. 1990. *Gender Trouble: Feminism and the Subversion of Identity*. London: Routledge.

Castles, S., and Miller, M. 1993. *The Age of Migration: International Population Movements in the Modern World*. New York: Guilford.

Central Bureau of Statistics. 2014. *The Ethiopian Population in Israel*. www.cbs.gov.il/reader/newhodaot/hodaa_template.html?hodaa=201511302 (accessed February 29, 2016).

Choo, H. Y., and Marx Ferree, M. 2010. "Practicing Intersectionality in Sociological Research: A Critical Analysis of Inclusion, Interactions, and Institutions in the Study of Inequalities." *Sociological Theory* 28: 129–49.

Cicurel, I., and Sharaby, R. 2007. "Women in the Menstruation Huts: Variations in Preserving Purification Customs Among Ethiopian Immigrants." *Journal of Feminist Studies in Religion* 23.2: 69–84.

Dahan-Kalev, H. 2014. "Paths to Middle-Class Mobility Among Second-Generation Moroccan Immigrant Women in Israel." *Journal of Modern Jewish Studies* 13.3: 465–66.

Dahan-Kalev, H., and Maor, M. 2015. "Skin Color Stratification in Israel Revisited." *Journal of Levantine Studies* 5.1: 9–33.

Dekel, T. 2011. "From First Wave to Third Wave Feminist Art in Israel: A Quantum Leap." *Israel Studies* 16.1: 149–78.

———. 2012. "Feminist Art Hitting the Shores of Israel: Three Case Studies in Impossible Times." *Frontiers: A Journal of Women Studies* 33.2: 111–28.

———. 2013. *Gendered: Art and Feminist Theory*. Newcastle, UK: Cambridge Scholars.

DeLaet, D. 1999. "Introduction: The Invisibility of Women in Scholarship on International Migration." In *Gender and Immigration*, ed. G. Kelson and D. DeLaet, 1–19. New York: New York University Press.

Demle, M. A. 2011. *Half Foreigners*. Holon: Orion (Hebrew).

Dill, B. 1983. "Race, Class, and Gender: Prospects for an All-Inclusive Sisterhood." *Feminist Studies* 9.1: 131–50.

Direktor, R. 2000. *Getting Dressed*. Exhibition catalog. Haifa: Haifa Museum of Art (Hebrew).

Donato, K., Abaccia, D., Holdaway, J., Manalansan, M., and Pessar, P. 2006. "A Glass Half Full? Gender and Migration Studies." *International Migration Review* 40.1: 3–26.

Ehrenreich, B., and Russell Hochschild, A. 2004. *Global Women: Nannies, Maids, and Sex Workers in the New Economy*. New York: Henry Holt.

El Or, T. 2006. *Reserved Seats: Gender, Ethnicity, and Religion in Contemporary Israel*. Tel Aviv: Am Oved (Hebrew).

Erlich, H. 2013. "Etiopia: chida bat shonot alpayim" [Ethiopia: A 2,000-Year-Old Enigma]. In *Ethiopia: The Land of Wonders* (exhibition catalog), ed. S. Turel, 25–37. Tel Aviv: Eretz Israel Museum (Hebrew).

Ernst, D. 2009. "The Meaning and Liberal Justifications of Israel's Law of Return." *Israel Law Review* 42.3: 564–602.

Fall, N. 2007. "Providing a Space of Freedom: Women Artists in Africa." In *Global Feminisms: New Directions in Contemporary Art*, ed. M. Reilly and L. Nochlin, 71–77. London: Merrell. blogs.fu-berlin.de/thesoapbox/files/2013/03/NGone-Fall-Providing-a-space-of-freedom.-Women-artists-from-Africa-2007.pdf (accessed January 1, 2014).

Fanon, F. 1967. *Black Skin, White Masks*, trans. C. Markmann. New York: Grove Press.

Foucault, M. 1980. "Prison Talk." In *Power/Knowledge: Selected Interviews and Other Writings, 1972–1977*, ed. C. Gordon, 37–54. Brighton, UK: Harvester Press.

Fuchs, E. 2014a. "The Evolution of Critical Paradigms in Israeli Feminist Scholarship: A Theoretical Model." In *Israeli Feminist Scholarship: Gender, Zionism, and Difference*, ed. E. Fuchs, 27–50. Austin: University of Texas Press.

———. 2014b. "Introduction." In *Israeli Feminist Scholarship: Gender, Zionism, and Difference*, ed. E. Fuchs, 1–25. Austin: University of Texas Press.

Fukuyama, F. 1989. "The End of History?" *The National Interest* 16 (summer): 3–18.

Funk, N., and Mueller, M., eds. 1993. *Gender, Politics, and Post-Communism: Reflections from Eastern Europe and the Former Soviet Union*. London: Routledge.

Galili, L., and Bronfman, R. 2013. *The Million That Changed the Middle East*. Tel Aviv: Matar (Hebrew).

Ghanem, H. 2008. "Mahu tzivo shel ha-or? Mabat biqorti al mischaqay tzeva" [What Is the Color of Skin? A Critical Look at Color Games]. In *Racism in Israel*, ed. Y. Shenhav and Y. Yona, 76–92. Jerusalem: Van Leer Institute (Hebrew).

Gitzin-Adiram, M., and Abir, L. 2007. *Meshane makom* [Changing Places]. Exhibition catalog. Bat Yam: Bat Yam Museum (Hebrew).

Glasner, A. 2005. "Mechira shel qlita le-lo astrategia" [The Cost of Unplanned Absorption]. *Eretz Acheret* 30: 43–47 (Hebrew).

Goffstein, A. 2013. "Alimut minit klapey mehagrot avoda be-yisrael be-re'i ha-halikh ha-plili" [Sexual Violence Toward Women Migrant Workers in Israel in Light of Criminal Procedure]. *Hamishpat* 17.1: 379–420 (Hebrew).

Golden, D. 2003. "A National Cautionary Tale: Russian Women Newcomers to Israel Portrayed." *Nations and Nationalism* 9.1: 83–104.

Gomel, E. 2006. *You and We: Russians in Israel*. Tel Aviv: Kinneret, Zmora-Bitan (Hebrew).

Gonchel, J. 2005. "Al tiruni she ani shcharchoret" [Look not Upon Me, Because I Am Black]. *Eretz Acheret* 30: 20–24 (Hebrew).

Gooldin, S., and Kemp, A. 2008. "Foreign and Fertile: The Biopolitics of Women Labor Migrants in Israel." In *Racism in Israel*, ed. Y. Shenhav and Y. Yonah, 258–86. Tel Aviv: Hakibbutz Hameuchad, and Jerusalem: Van Leer Institute (Hebrew).

Grewal, I. 2005. *Transnational America: Feminism, Diasporas, Neoliberalism*. Durham, NC: Duke University Press.

Guilat, Y. 2006. "Eyfo hayiten ume asiten: hasiach hamigdari baamanut bereshit shnot hatishim umekomo bebikoret ha'amanut beHa'aretz" [Where Have You Been and What Have You Been Doing? The Gendered Discourse in Art in the 1990s in the *Ha'aretz* Magazine]. *Israel* 9: 195–221 (Hebrew).

Guillaumin, Colette. 2003. *Racism, Sexism, Power, and Ideology*. London: Routledge. www.feministes-radicales.org/wp-content/uploads/2010/11/Colette-Guillaumin-Racism_Sexism_Power_and_Ideology.pdf (accessed February 10, 2016).

Hacker, D. 2009. "From the Moabite Ruth to Norly the Filipino: Intermarriage and Conversion in the Jewish Nation-State." In *Gendering Religion and Politics: Untangling Modernities*, ed. H. Herzog and A. Braude, 101–24. New York: Palgrave Macmillan.

———. 2012. "Religious Tribunals in Democratic States: Lessons from the Israeli Rabbinical Courts." *Journal of Law and Religion* 27.1: 59–81.

Hammerman, I. 2004. *In Foreign Parts: Trafficking Women in Israel.* Tel Aviv: Am Oved (Hebrew).

Harbon, C. 2012. "Diyur tzibori" [Public Housing]. In *The Political Lexicon of the Social Protest*, ed. A. Handel, 71–80. Tel Aviv: Hakibbutz Hameuchad (Hebrew).

Hasson, N. 2009. "Behirey hamishpetanim neged girush hazarim: busha ke'am vemedina" [Prominent Jurists Against Foreign Workers' Deportation: Shame as a Nation and a State]. *Haaretz*, September 11, 5 (Hebrew).

Herzog, E. 1998. *Immigrants and Bureaucrats: Ethiopians in an Israeli Absorption Center.* Oxford: Berghahn.

———. 2007. "About Bureaucracy and Ethnic Issues." In *To My Sister: Mizrahi Feminist Politics*, ed. Shlomit Lir, 131–39. Tel Aviv: Bavel Press (Hebrew).

Herzog, H. 2009. "Mabatim feministim" [Feminist Perspectives]. *Theory and Criticism* 34: 155–63 (Hebrew).

hooks, b. 1990. "Marginality as Site of Resistance." In *Out There: Marginalization and Contemporary Cultures*, ed. R. Ferguson, M. Gever, T. T. Minh-ha, and C. West, 341–43. Cambridge, MA: MIT Press.

Horowitz, T. 1998. "Yeladim ve-no'ar oleh be-ma'arekhet ha-chinukh: Hata'ama, chad leshoniut, chad kivuniut ve-stereotypiut" [Immigrant Children and Youth in the Education System: Assimilation, Monolingualism, Monodirectionality, and Stereotyping]. In *Profile of an Immigration Wave*, ed. M. Sikron and E. Leshem, 368–408. Jerusalem: Magnes Press (Hebrew).

Hsu, A. 2011. "You Have Your Own Country: Filipina Migrants 'Beyond Citizenship' in the Jewish State." PhD diss., London School of Economics.

Hughes, D. 2001. "The 'Natasha' Trade: Transnational Sex Trafficking." *National Institute of Justice Journal* 246 (January): 9–15.

Hujo, K., and N. Piper, eds. 2010. *South-South Migration.* Basingstoke, UK: Palgrave-Macmillan.

Huntington, S. 1997. *The Clash of Civilizations and the Remaking of World Order.* New York: Simon & Schuster.

Huss, E. 2010. "Shimush Bemechkar Mevusas Yetzira Miperspektive Bikortit" [Using Art Based Research, A Critical Perspective]. In *Nituach nitunim be-mchqar ikhuti* [The Analysis of Data in Qualitative Research], ed. L. Kasan and M. Kromer-Nevo, 305–22. Beersheba: Ben-Gurion University Press (Hebrew).

ILO (International Labor Office). 2004. *Toward a Fair Deal for Migrant Workers in the Global Economy*. Geneva: ILO. www.ilo.org/public/english/standards/relm/ilc/ilc92/pdf/rep-vi.pdf (accessed March 4, 2016).

Istuchina, A., and Zamir, I. 2012. *Doch madad ha-bitachon shel nashim: mimtza'im nivcharim* [Women's Security Index Report: Selected Findings]. Haifa: Women's Security Coalition (Hebrew). www.isha.org.il/upload/file/WSI-index-hebrew-arabic-russian1.pdf (accessed February, 12, 2013).

Kacen, L., and Shabtay, M. 2005. "Gevarim me-etiopia ve-nashim mi-yisrael" [Ethiopian Men and Israeli Women]. *Eretz Acheret* 30: 62–65 (Hebrew).

Kaplan, C., and Grewal, I. 1999. "Transnational Feminist Cultural Studies: Beyond the Marxism/Poststructuralism/Feminism Divides." In *Between Woman and Nation: Nationalism, Transnational Feminism, and the State*, ed. C. Kaplan, N. Alarcón, and M. Moallem, 349–64. Durham, NC: Duke University Press.

Katz-Freiman, Tami. 1994. *Meta Sex 94: Identity, Body, and Sexuality*. Bat Yam and Ein Harod: Museum of Ein Harod.

Kemp, A., and Raijman, R. 2008. *Migrants and Workers: The Political Economy of Labor Migration in Israel*. Tel Aviv: Hakibbutz Hameuchad (Hebrew).

Kempadoo, K., Sanghera, J., and Pattanaik, B., eds. 2005. *Trafficking and Prostitution Reconsidered: New Perspectives on Migration, Sex Work, and Human Rights*. London: Paradigm.

Kiblitskaya, M. 2000. "Russia's Female Breadwinners: The Changing Subjective Experience." In *Gender, State, and Society in Soviet and Post-Soviet Russia*, ed. S. Ashwin, 90–105. London: Routledge.

Kraft, D. 2013. "Aliya mi-tokh emuna" [Immigration on the Basis of Faith]. *Haaretz*, August 16: 8 (Hebrew).

Kristeva, J. 1991. *Strangers to Ourselves*. New York: Columbia University Press.

Lael, I. 2008. "Lo mi-kan ve-lo mi-sham" [Neither from Here or There]. *Hed Hachinukh* 82.6: 128–29 (Hebrew).

Leibowitz, I., Shower, N., and Kaufman, N. 2013. "Mehagrot, ovdot, menutzalot" [Women, Workers, Exploited]. *Haokets*, March 12. www.haokets.org/2013/03/12 (accessed March 7, 2016) (Hebrew).

Lemish, D. 2000. "The Whore and the Other: Israeli Images of Female Immigrants from the Former USSR." *Gender and Society* 14.2: 333–49.

Lerner, J., 2012. "Introduction: The Pragmatic Power of a Culture in Migration." In *Russians in Israel: The Pragmatics of Culture in Migration*, ed. J. Lerner and R. Feldhay, 20–47. Jerusalem: Van Leer Institute (Hebrew).

Lerner, J., and Feldhay, R., eds. 2012. *Russians in Israel: The Pragmatics of Culture in Migration*. Jerusalem: Van Leer Institute (Hebrew).

Lev Ari, L. 2012. "Does Gender Impact Second Generation Emigrants? Ethnic Identity and Identification Among Israeli Emigrants' Offspring." *Social Issues in Israel* 14: 208–36.

Levenkron, N., and Dahan, Y. 2003. *Women as Commodities: Trafficking in Women in Israel*. Tel Aviv: Hotline for Migrant Workers, Isha L'Isha, and Adva Center. adva.org/wp-content/uploads/2014/09/TraffickingReport 2003Engfinal.pdf (accessed March 12, 2016).

Lichotinsky, V. 2012. "Ze gam ha-shidur sheli" [It's My Broadcast Too]. *Haaretz*, July 31 (Hebrew). www.haaretz.co.il/opinions/1.1789516 (accessed February 27, 2016).

Lir, S. 2007. *To My Sister: Mizrahi Feminist Politics*. Tel Aviv: Bavel Press (Hebrew).

Lissyutkina, L. 1993. "Soviet Women at the Crossroads of Perestroika." In *Gender, Politics, and Post-Communism: Reflections from Eastern Europe and the Former Soviet Union*, ed. N. Funk and M. Mueller, 274–86. London: Routledge.

Lomsky-Feder, E., and Rapoport, T., eds. 2010. *Visibility in Immigration: Body, Gaze, Representation*. Jerusalem: Van Leer Institute (Hebrew).

Mahler, S., and Pessar, P. 2001. "Gendered Geographies of Power: Analyzing Gender Across Transnational Spaces." *Identities* 7.4: 441–59.

Maor, H. 2004. *Cosmopalit: Hishtakfut zehutam shel omanim mi-brit ha-mo'etzot le-she-avar be-omanut ha-yisraelit ha-akshavit* [Cosmo-Refugee: The Reflection of the Identity of FSU Migrants in Contemporary Israeli Art]. Exhibition catalog. Beersheba: University Gallery, Ben-Gurion University of the Negev (Hebrew).

Markovitch, D., and Alon, K. 2005. "Post kolonializm afriqa'i: Mabat acher al post-kolonializm" [African Post-Colonialism: A Different View on Post-Colonialism]. *Hakivun mizrah* 10: 5–10 (Hebrew).

Markus, R., ed. 2008. *Women Artists in Israel, 1920–1970*. Tel Aviv: Hakibbutz Hameuchad (Hebrew).

Marzel, S. R. 2008. "Amalanut nashit be-qehilot shulayim be-yisrael" [Female Handicraft in Marginal Communities in Israel]. In *Chatzrot ahoriot*, ed. Y. Bar-On and E. Terzi, 81–86. Jerusalem: Bezalel (Hebrew).

Meskimmon, M., and Rowe, D. C., eds. 2013. *Women, the Arts, and Globalization: Eccentric Experience*. Manchester, UK: Manchester University Press.

Michaeli, I. 2011. "Ha-hagira charuta al ha-guf" [Migration Is Engraved on the Body]. In *Women and Their Bodies: Our Bodies, Health, and Sexuality*, ed. T. Tamir, 38. Tel Aviv: Modan (Hebrew).

Minh-ha, T. 1989. *Women, Native, Other: Writing Postcoloniality and Feminism*. Bloomington: Indiana University Press.

Ministry of Industry, Trade, and Labor Report to the OECD. 2012. www.moital.gov.il/NR/exeres/4A75C33C-3C8A-4859-9EE9-76EAB8B2A1CC.htm (accessed March 9, 2016) (Hebrew).

Mizrachi, N., and Herzog, H. 2012. "Participatory Destigmatization Strategies Among Palestinian Citizens, Ethiopian Jews, and Mizrahi Jews in Israel." *Ethnic and Racial Studies* 35.3: 418–35.

Mohanty, C. T. 2003. *Feminism Without Borders: Decolonizing Theory, Practicing Solidarity*. Durham, NC: Duke University Press.

Momsen, J. 2004. *Gender and Development*. London: Routledge.

Mor, V. 2010. *The Scroll of Converts*. Jerusalem: Reuben Mass (Hebrew).

Morag-Talmon, P., and Atzmon, Y., eds. *Immigrant Women in Israel*. Jerusalem: Bialik Press (Hebrew).

Nagar-Ron, S., and Motzafi-Haller, P. 2011. "My Life? There Is not Much to Tell: On Voice, Silence, and Agency in Interviews with First-Generation Mizrahi Jewish Women Immigrants to Israel." *Qualitative Inquiry* 17.7: 653–63.

Nesher, T. 2012. "Atira: Etiopi'im nishlachim le-chinukh me'uchad le-lo siba" [Petition: Ethiopian Students Being Sent to Special-Needs Education for No Reason]. *Haaretz*, June 15: 10 (Hebrew).

Nisim, S., and Benjamin, O. 2010. "The Speech of Services Procurement: The Negotiated Order of Commodification and Dehumanization of Cleaning Employees." *Human Organization* 69.3: 221–32.

Nochlin, L. 1988 [1971]. "Why Have There Been No Great Women Artists?" In *Women, Art, and Power and Other Essays*, by L. Nochlin, 147–58. New York: Harper & Row. www.miracosta.edu/home/gfloren/nochlin.htm (accessed January 29, 2014).

Ofer, D. 2010. "Body and Soul: Youth Aliya Reflect on Themselves and Their Absorption, 1934–1951." In *Visibility in Immigration: Body, Gaze, Representation*, ed. E. Lumski-Feder and T. Rapoport, 99–139. Jerusalem: Van Leer Institute (Hebrew).

Parker, R., and Pollock, G. 1981. *Old Mistresses. Women, Art, and Ideology*. London: Harper Collins.

Peleg-Rotem, H. 2011. "Beyn shtey arim" [Between Two Cities]. *Globes*, December 6: 12 (Hebrew).

Perez, N. 2011. "Israel's Law of Return: A Qualified Justification." *Modern Judaism* 31.1: 59–84.

Philippov, M. 2010. *Ex-Soviets in the Israeli Political Space: Values, Attitudes, and Electoral Behavior*. Institute of Israel Studies, Research Paper 3.

Pilkington, H. 1992. "Behind the Mask of Soviet Unity: Realities of Women's Lives." In *Superwomen and the Double Burden: Women's Experience of Change in Central and Eastern Europe and the Former Soviet Union*, ed. C. Corrin, 180–235. London: Scarlet Press.

Piper, N. 2008. "International Migration and Gendered Axes of Stratification: Introduction." In *New Perspectives on Gender and Migration: Livelihood, Rights, and Entitlement*, ed. N. Piper, 1–18. New York: Routledge.

Porat, I. 2013. "Ani lo rotza le-hitlonen alav, raq techashavi li zquyot: 'Metaplot zarot' mutradot" [I Don't Want to Make a Complaint Against Him, Just Get Me My Rights: Harassed "Foreign" Caregivers]. PhD diss. Bar-Ilan University, Israel (in progress).

Raven, C., and Ringgold, F. 2004. *Faith Ringgold: A View from the Studio*. Boston: Bunker Hill.

Reider, D. 2013. "Izvu et ha-rusim" [Forget About the Russians]. *Haaretz*, May 14: 21 (Hebrew).

Reilly, M., and Nochlin, L., eds. 2007. *Global Feminisms: New Directions in Contemporary Art*. London and New York: Merrell Press.

Remennick, L. I. 1999. "Gender Implications of Immigration: The Case of Russian-Speaking Women in Israel." In *Gender and Immigration*, ed. G. A. Kelson and D. L. DeLaet, 163–85. New York: New York University Press.

———. 2003. "The 1.5 Generation of Russian Immigrants in Israel: Between Integration and Sociocultural Retention." *Diaspora* 12.1: 39–66.

———. 2007. *Russian Jews on Three Continents: Identity, Integration, and Conflict*. New Brunswick, NJ: Transaction.

Rogoff, I. 2000. *Terra Infirma: Geography's Visual Culture*. New York: Routledge.

Rosenthal, R. 2006. "Ha-oman 17: Tamara Brodinsky" [The Artist 17: Tamara Brodinsky]. *Walla!*, August 24. e.walla.co.il/?w=/274/963828 (accessed February 1, 2014) (Hebrew).

Rubinstein, T. 2013. "Ve-ani kvar hayiti me-kan" [I've Already Been from Here]. *Ha'oketz*, April 27 (Hebrew). www.haokets.org/2013/04/27 (accessed February 28, 2016).

Russell Hochschild, A. 2004. "Love and Gold." In *Global Women: Nannies, Maids, and Sex Workers in the New Economy*, ed. B. Ehrenreich and A. Russell Hochschild, 15–30. New York: Henry Holt.

Sabar, G. 2008. *"We Are Not Here to Stay": African Labor Migrants in Israel and Back to Africa.* Tel Aviv: Tel Aviv University Press (Hebrew).

———. 2010. *Dispatches from African History.* Tel Aviv: Open University and Ministry of Defense (Hebrew).

Sabar Friedman, G. 1989. "Religion and the Marxist State in Ethiopia: The Case of the Ethiopian Jews." *Religion, State, and Society* 17.3: 247–56.

Salamon, H. 1997. "Hitpatchuta shel tfisa giz'anit: Me-etiopia le-eretz ha-muvtachat" [The Development of a Racist View: From Ethiopia to the Promised Land]. *Jerusalem Studies* 15: 117–34 (Hebrew).

Salazar Parreñas, R. 2004. "The Care Crisis in the Philippines: Children and Transnational Families in the New Global Economy." In *Global Women: Nannies, Maids, and Sex Workers in the New Economy*, ed. B. Ehrenreich and A. Russell Hochschild, 39–54. New York: Henry Holt.

Sassen, S. 2004. "Global Cities and Survival Circuits." In *Global Women: Nannies, Maids, and Sex Workers in the New Economy*, ed. B. Ehrenreich and A. Russell Hochschild, 254–74. New York: Henry Holt.

Sela, M. 2011. "Charadatan ha-qiumit shel bubot al chut" [The Existential Fear of Puppets on a String]. *Haaretz* (*Musaf Galleriya*), October 6: 1–2 (Hebrew).

Shabtay, M. 2001. "Lechiot im zehut meyu'emet: Chavayat he-chayim im shoni be-tzeva or be-kerev tzi'irim u-mitbagrim yotzey etiopia be-yisrael" [Living with a Threatened Identity: The Experience of Life with a Different Color Among Ethiopian Youth and Adolescents in Israel]. *Megamot* 41.1–2: 97–112 (Hebrew).

———. 2006. *Yehudai Etiopia Mi'zera Israel* [Ethiopian Jews of Beta Israel Origin]. Tel Aviv: Lashon Tzeha Press (Hebrew).

Shalom, S. 2013. "Beta Israel: Origins and Religious Features." In *Ethiopia: The Land of Wonders* (exhibition catalog), ed. S. Turel, 53–63. Tel Aviv: Eretz Israel Museum (Hebrew).

Sheffi, S. 2010. "Ta'arukhat bogray musrara: Raq bishvil lekabel chibuq" [Musrara Graduates' Exhibition: Only to Get a Hug]. *Haaretz*, July 23: 17 (Hebrew).

———. 2012. "Pnei Tzalekey" [Scare Face]. *Haaretz*, March 2: 17 (Hebrew).

Shenhav, Y., and Yonah, Y. 2008. *Racism in Israel.* Tel Aviv: Hakibbutz Hameuchad, and Jerusalem: Van Leer Institute (Hebrew).

Shmueloff, M., Gorfinkel, B., and Herzog, O. 2007. "Le'aer al misdar ha'zihui" [To Undermine the Line-Up]. *Ka'Kivun Mizrah* 14: 6–11 (Hebrew).

Shohat, E., ed. 2006. *Taboo Memories, Diasporic Voices*. Durham, NC: Duke University Press.

Shuval, J., and Leshem, E. 1998. "The Sociology of Migration in Israel: A Critical View." In *Immigration to Israel: Sociological Perspectives*, ed. J. Shuval and E. Leshem, 3–50. New Brunswick, NJ: Transaction.

Sikron, M., and Leshem, E., eds. 1998. *Profile of an Immigration Wave: The Absorption Process of Immigrants from the Former Soviet Union, 1990–1995*. Jerusalem: Magnes Press (Hebrew).

Skeggs, B. 1997. *Formations of Class and Gender: Becoming Respectable*. London: Sage.

Slonim-Nevo, V., and Mirsky, J. 2002. "Adolescents as Migrants." *Panim* 19: 106–11 (Hebrew).

Smooha, S. 2008. "The Immigration to Israel: A Comparison of the Failure of the Mizrahi Immigration of the 1950s with the Success of the Russian Immigrants of the 1990s." *Journal of Israeli History* 27.1: 1–27.

Sperber, D. 2012. "'Ha-muqtza': Nida, tuma'a ve-tehora be-omanut yehudit feministit" [The Outcast: Menstruation, Impurity, and Purity in Feminist Jewish Art]. In *Matronita: omanut yehudit feministi.* (exhibition catalog), ed. D. Liss and D. Sperber, 87–110. Tel Aviv: Mishkan le-omanut, Ein Harod (Hebrew).

Spivak, G. C. 1988. "Can the Subaltern Speak? In *Marxism and the Interpretation of Culture*, ed. C. Nelson and L. Grossman, 24–58. London: Macmillan.

———. 1998. "Responsibility." In *Gendered Agents: Women and Institutional Knowledge*, ed. S. Mariniello and P. Bove, 19–66. Durham, NC: Duke University Press.

Steir, H., and Levanon, V. 2003. "Finding an Adequate Job: Employment and Income of Recent Immigrants to Israel." *International Migration* 41.2: 81–107.

Sweifach, J. 2005. "Who Is a Jew?" *Journal of Religion and Spirituality in Social Work: Social Thought* 24.4: 89–102.

Swirksi, M., and Swirski, B. 2002. *Ha-yehudim yotzey etiopia be-yisrael: Diyur, ta'asuqa, chinuch* [Ethiopian Jewish Immigrants in Israel: Housing, Employment, Education]. Tel Aviv: Adva Center (Hebrew).

Tantzer, A. 2012. "Second-Class Citizens." *Haaretz* (*Musaf de'ot*), March 11: 16 (Hebrew).

Teferra, A. 2013. "An Overview of Ethiopian Languages and Cultures." In *Ethiopia: The Land of Wonders* (exhibition catalog), ed. S. Tural, 39–51. Tel Aviv: Eretz Israel Museum (Hebrew).

Transparency International. 2012. *Transparency International Corruption Perceptions Index 2012.* Berlin: Transparency International. www.ey.com/Publication/vwLUAssets/2012_TI_CPI/$FILE/2012%20TI%20CPI.pdf.

Turel, S. 2013. "Etiopia: Mabat qaleidesqopi" [Ethiopia: A Kaleidoscopic View]. In *Ethiopia: The Land of Wonders* (exhibition catalog), ed. S. Turel, 13–22. Tel Aviv: Eretz Israel Museum (Hebrew).

Tuval, S. 2004. "Social Representation of Inclusion, Exclusion, and Stratification in School as Factors in Channeling Children to a Special Education Career." PhD diss., Ben-Gurion University (Hebrew).

UN Population Fund. 2008. *Gender Inequality and Women's Empowerment: Ethiopian Society of Population Studies—In-Depth Analysis of the Ethiopian Demographic and Healthy Survey, 2005.* Addis Ababa: United Nations Population Fund. ethiopia.unfpa.org/drive/Gender.pdf (accessed January 29, 2014).

Wagner, R. 2010. "Women Migrant Workers." *Mafteach: Lexical Review of Political Thought* 1: 61–90. mafteakh.tau.ac.il/en/2010–01/06/ (accessed January 2, 2014).

Weiler-Polak, D. 2011. "Ovdim zarim mitlonanim al hatrada ve-hitolalut, ha-ma'asaqim le ne'anshim" [Foreign Workers Complain of Harassment and Abuse, Employers not Punished]. *Haaretz*, November 28: 10 (Hebrew).

Weisberg, H. 2012. "Tachtit shuq ha-avoda: Etiopim—meqablim ha-sekhar ha-namikh be-yisrael" [Bottom of the Labor Market: Ethiopians Earn the Lowest Wage in Israel]. *The Marker*, March 5. www.themarker.com/career/1.1656489 (accessed February 29, 2016) (Hebrew). [English edition: "Ethiopian Immigrants Earning 30%–40% Less than Arabs," *Haaretz*, March 5, 2014; www.haaretz.com/business/ethiopian-immigrants-earning-30-40-less-than-arabs-1.416551 (accessed February 29, 2016).]

Wertzberg, R. 2003. *Mismach odot qehilat yotzey etiopia: Tmunat matzav adkanit, pa'arim ve-ta'anot ke-aflayah* [Document Regarding the Ethiopian Immigrant Community: Picture of the Current Situation, Gaps, and Claims of Discrimination]. Jerusalem: Knesset Israel (Hebrew).

Willen, S., ed. 2007. *Transnational Migration to Israel in Global Comparative Context.* Lanham, MD: Lexington.

Women's Affairs Office, Federal Democratic Republic of Ethiopia. 1998. *Women in Ethiopia: National Policy on Ethiopian Women.* Geneva: World Bank. www.ethioembassy.org.uk/fact%20file/a-z/women-1.htm (accessed January 29, 2014).

The World Bank. 2011. *Migration and Remittance Factbook 2011*. data.worldbank.org/data-catalog/migration-and-remittances (accessed March 3, 2016).

Wurgaft, N. 2006. *Police! Open up! Migrant Workers in Israel*. Tel Aviv: Am Oved (Hebrew).

Yakir, E. 2005. "Lehitkofef keday la-qum me-chadash" [To Stoop in Order to Stand Up Again]. *Eretz Acheret* 20: 32–36 (Hebrew).

Yanai, N., and Rappoport, T. 2001. "Nida u-le'umiyut: Guf ha-isha be-text" [Menstruation and Nationalism: The Body of the Woman in the Text]. In *Ha-tishma qoli? Yitzugim shel nashim ba-tarbut ha-yisraelit* [Will You Listen to My Voice? Representations of Women in Israeli Culture], ed. Y. Atzmon, 213–24. Jerusalem: Van Leer Institute (Hebrew).

Yuval-Davis, N. 1997. *Gender and Nation*. London: Sage.

———. 1999. "Multi-Layered Citizenship in the Age of 'Globalization.'" *International Feminist Journal of Politics* 1.1: 119–36.

Yuval-Davis, N., Anthias, F., and Kofman, E. 2005. "Secure Borders and Safe Haven and the Gendered Politics of Belonging: Beyond Social Cohesion." *Ethnic and Racial Studies* 28.3: 513–35.

Ziv, E. 2012. "Insidious Trauma." *Mafteach* 5: 55–73 (Hebrew).

Index

www.ingramcontent.com/pod-product-compliance
Lightning Source LLC
LaVergne TN
LVHW010448080826
844660LV00027B/1235

* 9 7 8 0 8 1 4 3 4 2 5 0 3 *